Praise for
HACKING SCHOOL CULTURE

"Teaching is meaningful and demanding. *Hacking School Culture: Designing Compassionate Classrooms* is a way to bring out the best in your students—and yourself. Through time-tested and research-driven approaches to flourishing, this book is chock-full of easy-to-implement actions that are kind to you, the students, and to the environment you're creating in the classroom. Try these simple ideas to enliven and energize the teaching experience."

—**MEGAN MCDONOUGH,** CEO and Co-Founder, Wholebeing Institute

"The world needs individuals that are compassionate, self-directed, and committed to contributing to the common good. For our youngest members of society, schools are a major institution in which they acquire and enhance knowledge, skills, and dispositions. Unfortunately, most schools focus on academic content rather than ensuring each student is provided an authentic learning experience in a culture that is inclusive, safe, and engaging.

"The *Hacking School Culture* co-authors guide us on a journey of 10 connected themes to create and sustain compassionate classrooms that are motivational and educational for each student. Each theme provides a comprehensive description and alignment with positive student development, strategies based on evidence, and immediate and long-term actions and strategies to overcome challenges. The themes are augmented with quotes and personal stories bringing to life the need for compassion as both a personal attribute and a characteristic of the school's environment."

—**TERRY PICKERAL,** President, Cascade Educational Consultants

"For teachers to continue to grow as professionals, *Hacking School Culture* is a practical guide to help them improve the classroom experience for students. Readers will walk away inspired to practice and implement a more empathic approach that goes beyond teaching subject matter. This book provides useful 'how-to's' that aid in reframing how and why we think about our roles as educators to build more meaningful and impactful relationships with students. To this day, I remember those teachers who not only taught me the curriculum, but who took the time to understand me and shaped who I am today."

—**TERRY L. JACKSON, ED.D.**, The George Washington University, Office of Special Education Programs/U.S.DOE

"Ellen and Angela lead the reader to practiced and doable strategic events that go beyond the 'hope for an osmotic transformation' and into the realm of viable and responsible action. The skill sets and values presented within this book, when practiced with fidelity, positively change school culture, advance understanding, cultivate a sense of validation and self-worth, leading to an empowerment that is often missing in today's world."

—**LAWRENCE FELDMAN, PH.D.**, School Board of Miami-Dade County

"'What if practicing empathy was the first step to designing education?' Thus begins Ellen Feig Gray and Angela Stockman's brilliant new book, *Hacking School Culture*. This courageous and heartfelt guide for parents and educators presents a blueprint for implementing compassion within any classroom. Their expertise and extensive research are evident in every page of this clear and concise book. As a developmental pediatrician for the past 30 years, I have witnessed first-hand the rising epidemic of alienation, anxiety and ADHD that has resulted from an educational system that promotes

HACKING
SCHOOL
CULTURE

productivity over process. I have also seen the power empathy has to transform the way we pay attention. Using real life examples throughout this book, Ellen and Angela provide ways you can become a 'design thinker,' someone who can energize the classroom through compassion. In so doing, they offer a path of transformation that raises the dignity of each student while supporting our teachers' enormous task of inspiring growth through connection. This book is destined to become an important resource for anyone involved in the education of children in today's culture."

> —STEPHEN SCOTT COWAN, M.D., Author of *Fire Child, Water Child: How Understanding the Five Types of ADHD Can Help You Improve Your Child's Self-Esteem and Attention*

"*Hacking School Culture: Designing Compassionate Classrooms* is a valuable addition to the HACK Learning Series. It provides concrete support and suggestions for teachers to improve their interactions with their students at the same time they enrich their own professional experiences. The hacks encourage teachers to regard their students with compassion and empathy, respecting both their individuality and their strengths as a productive way of redesigning the classroom for better learning. This approach not only leads to better educational outcomes for students, it also stems burn-out through more meaningful professional experiences for teachers. Although primarily aimed at K-12 classrooms, the authors' insightful suggestions have given me, a veteran college professor, new insights into positive classroom dynamics which I have already begun to incorporate into my classes."

> —LOUISE HAINLINE, PH.D., Professor of Psychology, Brooklyn College of CUNY

HACKING SCHOOL CULTURE

Designing Compassionate Classrooms

Angela Stockman
Ellen Feig Gray

PUBLICATIONS

These books are available at special discounts when purchased in quantity for use as premiums, promotions, fundraising, and educational use. For inquiries and details, contact us at www.hacklearning.org

Published by Times 10
Highland Heights, OH
Times10Books.com

Project Management by Kelly Schuknecht
Cover and Interior Design by Kellie Emery, Koehler Studios
Editing by Joe Coccaro and Hannah Woodlan, Koehler Studios

Library of Congress Cataloging-in-Publication Data is available.
ISBN: 978-1-948212-04-5

First Printing: May, 2018

Contents

PREFACE

HOW IS IT that two middle aged, middle class, white women from Buffalo, New York and Miami, Florida came to write a book about creating compassionate classrooms? We began by building a long friendship around our experiences as passionate learners, teachers, and supporters of parents and educators who strive to create schools that recognize and honor children, individually, for who they really are. The last three decades of our lives have provided vast and varied experiences that have informed our perspectives.

Still, as middle aged and middle class white women, we knew that our perspectives were limited and that in order to write a book of this nature, we would need to seek a diverse set of teachers who would champion our intentions while deepening our self awareness and shining a bright light on our potential blind spots. Many thanks to Jennifer Borgioli Binis, Daniel and Jane Atchison Nevel, Avis and Larry Feldman, Kristal Hickmon, Louise Hainline, Tal Ben-Shahar, Maria Sirois, Megan McDonough, Stephen Cowan, Alison Deutsch, Wendy Gordon, Heather French, Laura Frohman, Lori Moldovan, Megha Nancy Buttenheim, Missy Brown, Susan Kelly, Che Amirault, the Moon Dancers, the First Born Angel Dancers, and the CiPP community for inspiring, informing, and at times, challenging our thinking over the years.

We also owe a debt of gratitude to Sherri Spelic, a graduate of the Teachers College, Columbia University, editor of Identity, Education, and Power, and a Physical Education Specialist at the American International School, Vienna, as well as Rachel Fix Dominguez, a graduate of the Harvard University Graduate School of Education and the University of Buffalo and an education researcher with the Research Foundation of the State University of New York. These women made a close and very thoughtful study of this manuscript, and this helped us clarify our thinking and consider the intended and unintended consequences of the ways we chose to communicate about compassion.

We're grateful to you for reading too and for taking an interest in this topic. We imagine that many of our readers are parents and educators who are living the realities that we speak to in this book and doing hard but very good work with great intentions. Please help us learn more about this world that our children will inherit. Share your thinking. Push ours. We still have so much to learn about creating compassionate classrooms and schools, and we'd love to connect with you.

You'll find us on Twitter: we're @AngelaStockman and @EllenFeigGray there. And we invite you to subscribe to our community at compassionateclassrooms.org. See you there.

INTRODUCTION

One Learner, One Teacher, One Classroom at a Time

The most crucial use of knowledge and education
is to understand the importance of developing a good heart.
—HIS HOLINESS THE 14TH DALAI LAMA OF TIBET

W E WEREN'T AWARE of it at the time, but we started writing this book when we first met 10 years ago. Angela's then 10-year-old daughter had launched a blogging project to encourage and document how everyday people were making a difference in their communities in only 25 days. Ellen's then 15-year-old son had formed a nonprofit to motivate young people to vote for the first time and become informed about candidates and issues important to them. As their parents, we were committed to supporting our children and enabling them to flourish. We allowed them to follow their passions and put their projects first, sometimes at the expense of their school obligations. Some of their teachers and administrators were not aligned with our approach, but thankfully many saw the bigger picture.

The most sensitive educators took the time to see who our kids really were. They recognized their needs and understood that the authentic learning experiences that they created for themselves would serve them well in both the short and long term. And they were right. Ten years later, each of our kids is a thriving and accomplished young adult, doing good work in this world. And the teachers who supported them best continue to do the same for others.

Many of them are worried, though. In the years since our children were young, they've watched their students exhibit higher rates of anxiety and depression. They've become more aware of the traumas their students bring to school. They've grown concerned about the isolating power of technology. They've witnessed a dramatic increase in hate crimes, mass shootings, and incidents of sexual harassment on college campuses and in the workplaces they're preparing their students to enter.

As a teacher and professional learning facilitator, Angela meets colleagues like these in classrooms every day, and Ellen encounters them in the parenting workshops and coaching sessions she leads. This book is the result of the personal and professional journey we are both living, as we observe and investigate the role that compassion plays in our ability to thrive and help students do the same.

We started imagining: What if our kids weren't outliers in a system that chose to recognize their unique interests and needs? What if that spirit was not reactive but intentionally built into the school culture? We wondered: How might we create systems where the things that students and teachers wanted most informed school vision and comprised the core of their learning? What if practicing empathy was the first step to designing their education?

Experience has taught us that students' success and teachers' job satisfaction are necessarily dependent upon an atmosphere of emotional safety and positive social relationships. It's all about connection. It's about being seen. We also believe that the goal of education is to ignite people's natural motivation to learn and grow, not only to reach their human potential, but to help them become increasingly human as well.

How might we become more human?

How might we help our students do the same?

We feel that compassion is key. Traditional definitions of the word speak to suffering, pity, and mercy. Dictionaries frame *compassion* as the desire to ease the pain that others experience. And empathy is defined by the ability to share others' feelings. We believe that being compassionate toward another doesn't always have to be a response to their pain, though. Everyone deserves compassion, whether or not they are suffering.

Many researchers equate compassion with open-heartedness. In addition to responding to others' pain and suffering with sensitivity, we also want to practice compassion when others experience joy and even great accomplishment. Some of the loneliest people in the world are those we put on pedestals. We've learned that it's important to treat joyful and accomplished people with as much consideration as those who experience pain and suffering. Surely, our own kids were not suffering, but they still needed friends, teachers, school administrators, and community members who respected their ambitions, believed in them, and recognized that achieving a dream can be a frightening thing, and that in order to do so, things are often lost along the way. Joy and success are actually quite complex. While it's easy to have compassion for those who struggle, practicing it in the face of someone's success requires a depth of understanding that is often hard to find.

Our working definition of compassion broadens its meaning beyond the component of suffering and necessarily includes action. More than merely feeling for someone who is in pain, we frame compassion as action. Specifically: behaving in a kind, understanding, and caring manner, regardless of what we might know or assume about a person's experiences or their interpretation of them.

According to the Glossary of Education Reform, the essential components of school culture are the beliefs, relationships, perceptions, attitudes, and written and unwritten rules inside of the system. The quality of the spaces that students learn in and the emotional safety they feel within those spaces contribute greatly as well. Compassionate schools value racial, ethnic, linguistic, and cultural diversity. They recognize the strengths that those with physical and mental disabilities possess as well, and they seek their contributions. Compassionate schools shape graduates who adopt these values as well.

Our 10 principles, which apply to children and adults, are defined in image I.1.

The Principles of Compassionate Classrooms

1. Compassion is requisite to learning.

2. Communities that flourish are founded on compassion.

3. In order to grow compassionate students, we must help them take risks and experience vulnerability.

4. Compassion inspires us to see people in all of their complexity, rather than sorting them into categories that diminish them.

5. The seeds of compassion must be planted in the classroom and tended to by the entire system.

6. All human beings are deserving of compassion, even those who are not experiencing suffering.

7. Compassion is a disposition that can be cultivated through explicit instruction and intentional practice.

8. Practicing compassion fosters resilience.

9. Compassion thrives in environments that give people permission to be human.

10. Creativity is ignited through compassionate inquiry.

Image I.1: Our 10 Principles

Our research has taught us that empathy and compassion are uniquely human character strengths that we all possess, and we can harness them at any time. And the field of positive education is demonstrating that empathy and compassion can be taught and cultivated, at home and inside of our communities. These are ancient teachings that most spiritual practices and religions share. They're also grounded in science. Even Charles Darwin, in developing the theory of evolution, observed that our neurological system needed to evolve in order to be able to recognize and respond to the needs of our offspring. If we were not able to access empathy and compassion, we humans would not have survived.

These understandings underpin design thinking, a creative approach that inspires us to make things that solve others' problems, meet their needs, and serve their interests. Rather than blindly lifting and dropping prefabricated practices and curriculum onto their students, compassionate teachers empathize with learners as they define, prototype, test, and evolve their curriculum, assessments, and instructional practices. Design thinking invites experimentation and encourages the acceptance of failure. It fosters learning and growth, academically, personally, and professionally. We believe that it has the potential to create cultural shifts inside of classrooms and school systems as well, as it thrives in communities that are diverse, connected, collaborative, and human-centered.

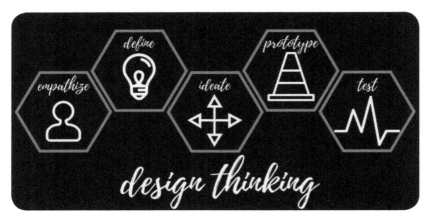

Image I.2: **Defining Design Thinking**

Currently, there are a few social emotional initiatives that have positive impacts on school culture. These programs are typically adopted by school leaders who facilitate them from the top down. However, we believe that compassionate schools find their roots inside of classrooms, with teachers who practice self-care and help their students do the same. They listen and strive to understand their students rather than merely evaluating or, worse, judging them. They model compassion for others, and they coach the development of powerful practices that shift school culture one student and classroom at a time.

Most agree that our primary job as teachers and parents is to prepare our children for future success. We are living in a time of technological and entrepreneurial opportunity. It's difficult to predict how employment landscapes might shift over time, but regardless of this uncertainty, there are certain character strengths that most employers will continue to value: curiosity, creativity, initiative, multidisciplinary thinking, teamwork, and empathy. These are uniquely human qualities, and we have the ability to design classroom experiences that teach, foster, and hone these strengths as we help our students acquire knowledge and sharpen their skills.

And who are we, anyway? Angela is a teacher, a writer, a writing coach, a professional learning facilitator, and a design-thinking enthusiast. Ellen is a psychology and communications researcher, a writer, a parent mentor, and a lifelong student of developmental and positive psychology. She is well-versed in the science of happiness and takes a strengths-based approach when helping others cultivate their own well-being and their relationships with others.

Like you, we've grappled with the tensions that arise inside of classrooms and schools that lack compassion. We've tried and failed a thousand times as parents and practitioners who are eager to prevent and repair the damage caused by bullying, cultural incompetence, and teacher burnout, which often results from compassion fatigue. We've dealt with these realities on deeply personal levels, and while we've gained a lot of perspective, we know we don't have all of the answers yet.

So, we offer no simple solutions or silver bullets, only an invitation to start better conversations about things that matter. Join us as we seek to understand and create compassionate classrooms and schools.

GROW YOUR OWN

Developing Self-Compassion First

*The curious paradox is that when I accept
myself just as I am, then I can change.*
—CARL ROGERS, HUMANISTIC PSYCHOLOGIST, PSYCHOTHERAPY RESEARCHER

THE PROBLEM: TEACHERS ARE VULNERABLE TO COMPASSION FATIGUE

THE TEACHING PROFESSION in the United States has an attrition rate that is 8 percent greater than other professions, and twice that of other high-performing countries such as Finland or Singapore. Over the last decade, thousands of US teachers have called it quits well before retirement age. Although there are many reasons for this phenomenon, many teachers claim that the main causes for their burnout include being underpaid, underappreciated, undervalued, and excluded from processes that define how they teach and evaluate their students.

Teachers are the ultimate caregivers. And we all know that when caregivers neglect themselves, they become depleted and, ultimately, unable to care for anyone effectively. That is why it is critical that teachers and school leaders, who spend their days caring for the hearts and minds of their students, and their nights preparing to care for them all over again the next day, build in ways to take care of themselves.

It's easy to suggest going to the spa, getting a massage, taking a yoga class, eating better, getting more sleep, or taking a vacation. All of these ideas are good, but unless any of these practices become habits, they will not lead to lasting positive transformation or burnout prevention. We believe that in order to truly understand what other people need and to act compassionately toward others, we have to begin by caring for ourselves.

Who we are? What do we need? What do we value? What makes us . . . us? These may seem like supercilious questions, but if we're to sustain our passions as well as our energy for our students, we've learned that we must be clear about the answers. When Angela discusses burnout with teachers, many of them mention the sense of isolation they feel inside of their classrooms and schools. They often speak to the disconnect between who they are and what they've become as teachers over time. They mention the troubling consequences of testing and flawed evaluation systems. They speak about poor leadership. They struggle with the rapidly changing landscape of our country and our world. Many of them suffer under the scrutiny of colleagues who do not share their values or appreciate their pedagogy. Teachers can be unkind to one another, especially when they feel insecure.

Teachers need to be seen and heard, not only by their administrators and colleagues and students, but especially by themselves. Those who feel invisible or, worse, unaccepted find it almost impossible to maintain their appreciation for their work and the opportunities for growth that teaching can provide. People can't learn when they're afraid, and too many use fear as a motivator in our field. It takes a great deal of strength to admit when we are frightened. It takes even more to own our inadequacies and our part in any problem. Just as quickly as we recognize uncomfortable feelings, we often shrug them off. Few of us are very good at accepting how we feel, and this is where the real work begins.

When we are vulnerable with our students, they respect us for it. It's one way we become more human.

It's impossible to create compassionate classrooms for our students if we aren't cultivating compassion for ourselves.

Self-empathy involves acknowledging our feelings, both good and bad. When we allow ourselves to experience all of our emotions, even the ones we aren't proud of, and let them flow through us instead of blocking them or wallowing in the negative, we're more comfortable helping others do the same. This is what makes a teacher most powerful: the ability to care for themselves so well that they recognize the needs of their students. This kind of wholeheartedness is nourishment for the soul, and it does powerful things for the brain as well.

Whole-hearted teachers acknowledge that sometimes we will fail, feel frustrated, suffer losses, and come up against obstacles. Sometimes, we will lose it. We'll lose ourselves. We'll lose our students, too. If we are kind to ourselves, rather than resorting to pity, self-indulgence, or comparison, we can find the courage to share our struggles openly and hit the reset button. And this, in and of itself, is transformational. When we are vulnerable with our students, they respect us for it. It's one way we become more human. It's how we give them permission to do the same, too.

People who are gentle with themselves tend to be less anxious and depressed than others. They are also less likely to suffer from compassion fatigue. Instead, they experience satisfaction, higher energy, and greater happiness. Gentle people are strong enough to show up in big and often bold ways for their students. This elevates the students' confidence. It deepens their gratitude as well.

How do we practice self-compassion? Kristin Neff, PhD, a compassion researcher, author, and associate professor at the University of Texas at Austin's Department of Educational Psychology, suggests that we begin by recognizing and then silencing the critics who live inside of our heads. We need to be kind to ourselves, rather than harshly critical or judgmental. Fostering deeper connections with others is another self-compassion practice, and so is making an accurate assessment of our own experiences rather than ignoring or exaggerating our pain and suffering.

That sounds all well and good, but how do we get there? By designing our lives around practices that deepen our self-awareness and abilities to practice self-care. After all, the notion of practicing is necessarily iterative. In this case, our goal is to not become perfect, but to become more resilient and better able to handle all of our emotions, even the difficult ones, when they present themselves. These are the steps you can take to become gentler with yourself. This is the best way to begin creating a compassionate classroom and school.

◦ **WHAT YOU CAN DO TOMORROW** ◦

As Hack Learning authors, our job is to transform complex ideas into actionable plans and weighty theories into simple approaches that can help you—teachers and school leaders with very full lives—create meaningful change. Know that we have sampled these hacks from a deep exploration of the research on positive psychology, compassion, and careful studies of ancient wisdom. You will find references to this work and downloadable tools that will help you apply it by following the QR codes at the end of every hack in this book. There, you will find supplemental resources folders that will expand your learning and work.

And remember: The ideas that follow are not a prescription, but simple suggestions for you to try.

- **EMPATHIZE WITH YOURSELF.** In order to become other-centered, we need to connect to ourselves by assessing our well-being at a particular time, in a nonjudgmental fashion. There are many ways to tune into ourselves. A useful tool that has worked for Ellen and many of her colleagues in positive psychology and education is the SPIRE check-in.

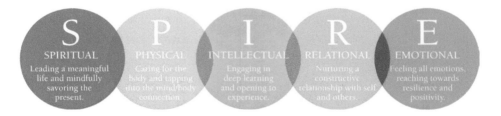

Image 1.1: The SPIRE Model of Whole-Being Wellness

Developed at the Wholebeing Institute, the SPIRE model of well-being allows us to take a reading of how we are doing in each of the five aspects of our daily lives: **S**piritually, **P**hysically, **I**ntellectually, **R**elationally, and **E**motionally. The SPIRE check-in is a moment-in-time evaluation where we ask "What is my experience now?" and we use our self-reflections to consider "How do I want to be?" It can be practiced easily at any time by using the printable protocol that can be found in the supplemental resources folder for this hack. Note: This is not an assessment that is intended to be scored, graded, or serve as a self-critical evaluation. It is a reading to be used as an opportunity to tweak your well-being practices.

- **SET AN INTENTION FOR YOUR DAY.** By setting an intention we are bringing our attention and awareness to a quality or virtue we want to cultivate. Intentions give us guidance on the direction we would like to take in our personal growth and development, and they are always positive. We might intend to be more forgiving of ourselves or others, to act with kindness, or even to make someone smile. Intentions are different than goals, which are specific and prescribe concrete action or results. Rather, intentions are more like dispositions to work toward. Intentions take us in the general direction of where we would like to go, based on the needs and desires of who we are designing for, leaving open the possibilities for how to get there. So, we may set an intention to be open-hearted. That means we will open our hearts to ourselves and others in the face of suffering and also in the face of joy and other positive and pleasurable emotions.

- **BE PRESENT, BE MINDFUL, AND BREATHE.** According to the wisdom traditions, as well as a large body of Western research studies, one of the best ways to tune into ourselves and cultivate self-compassion is to practice mindfulness. Mindfulness meditation helps us to be present as we focus on our breathing. Mindful breathing practices can be done while sitting still, or during walking meditation. Loving-kindness meditation has been shown to be particularly effective in building compassion, as it centers our attention around offering mettā— repeating phrases such as "May you be happy, may you be peaceful, may you live with ease, may you be joyful," sending well wishes to others and to ourselves.

When we turn our minds to a single point of reference and simply notice the content of our thoughts without identifying or investing in them, we enter a meditative state. We meditate in order to relax and deepen our capacity for compassion, love, patience, and even forgiveness. Meditation builds energy by calming our mind, body, and spirit. It's been proven to ease physical ailments as well, including chronic pain and high blood pressure. Practicing meditation will foster resilience and sustain your energy as you support your students on their own journeys toward compassionate living.

You'll find resources and tools for beginning or enriching your meditation and mindful breathing practices in the supplemental resources folder for this hack, including five simple exercises by global spiritual leader Thich Nhat Hanh, as well as loving-kindness meditation and other breathing techniques.

- **PRACTICE GRATITUDE.** Expressing gratitude and appreciation is one of the best ways to cultivate your overall happiness and well-being. It's equally important to appreciate your own strengths— the things you have to offer this world and what's working in your life. There are many ways to practice gratitude and appreciation, including keeping a journal and simply writing down three good things that happened today, or five things you're grateful for. "Appreciating something also causes it to grow," suggests Tal Ben-Shahar, PhD, co-founder of the Wholebeing Institute, a former Harvard professor, author of several books on happiness, and Ellen's positive psychology teacher. So, when you focus on what's working in your personal and professional life, the good appreciates and your capacity for self-compassion grows. And when you appreciate the good, your tendency to judge yourself negatively diminishes and your inner critic naturally falls quiet.

- **GIVE YOURSELF PERMISSION TO BE HUMAN.** This means giving ourselves the freedom to experience a full range of human emotions, whether positive and pleasurable, or negative and uncomfortable, and to acknowledge that we all share common emotional experiences as part of the human species. When we suppress, ignore, or deny emotions such as anger, sadness, jealousy, or frustration, they only intensify. When we understand that all of our feelings are normal and natural, and we let our emotions flow through us, we lay the foundation for enjoying greater happiness and life satisfaction. Giving ourselves permission to be human is not resigning ourselves to feeling negative emotions, but instead actively accepting whatever we feel, and choosing appropriate action in response. And let's not forget to allow ourselves to enjoy the pleasurable emotions too, such as the joy we share with others when we feel connected to one another in our common experience.

In addition to allowing ourselves to feel the full range of human emotions, we need to acknowledge that no one is perfect, or should aspire to perfection. As the saying goes, "Learn to fail or fail to learn." When we design our lives, we must be willing to try things that may work and some that may not, mustering the courage to be vulnerable and to own our imperfections. When we embrace our imperfections, we can be truly authentic and avoid the exhaustion that comes from trying to be perfect. And we can even fail our way to success if we reframe our mistakes as opportunities and part of an ongoing learning process. When we are intrinsically motivated by curiosity and a desire to improve, we challenge ourselves rather than avoiding mistakes at all costs. This is how we practice self-compassion. In the supplemental resources folder for Hack 1, you will find a guided meditation by Tal Ben-Shahar specifically designed to help you focus on giving yourself permission to be human.

◦ A BLUEPRINT FOR FULL IMPLEMENTATION ◦

It is well documented that in order to create lasting personal change or sustainable systemic transformation we need to create new habits in the behavioral, cognitive, and affective realms. That is, we need to act differently, think differently, and feel differently than we do in our current patterns. And the good news is that making a change in our behavior will necessarily influence our thoughts, attitudes and feelings. And it works in multiple and reciprocal ways: Our thoughts affect our emotions, our emotions affect our behavior, and our behavior affects our thoughts. Real change is difficult, but if we make small changes for the better over time, or as the Japanese say, take *kaizen* (small, gradual, and methodical) steps, we can achieve positive transformation.

Step 1. Create a world of possibility.

There are infinite ways to transform your life positively. What's most exciting is that your transformation is completely in your control— you get to choose what's good for you, what you like, what works for you, what's not working, and what compassion-building practices you'd like to become habits. Among the practices that we can try: blocking out time to take a walk each day, trading hair tips with a friend, hitting the nail salon, cooking yourself a nourishing meal or indulging in a decadent dessert, engaging in mindfulness meditation, going out dancing, singing with your church choir, studying Bible passages, meeting friends for a beverage and a few good laughs, writing thank-you letters, noticing three good things, doing yoga, taking in a show, scrapbooking, and even coloring. The sky's the limit—as long as it nurtures your overall well-being and increases your tendency to be compassionate toward yourself and others.

Step 2: Challenge yourself.

This is your chance to try something new, or to start a ritual that you've been thinking about but haven't experienced on a regular basis . . . yet. Choose a practice you'd like to try, and give yourself a 30-day challenge. There is some research to support the notion that it takes at least double that to create a new habit, but one month is a good amount of time to try out something new to see if it works for you. We have provided a 30-day challenge form in the supplemental resources folder for this hack.

On a personal note: When Ellen set an intention to experience more joy and have more fun in her life, she challenged herself to something she always loved to do—dance! She danced for about 30 minutes for a 30-day period and noticed an overall lift in her mood.

Because she found a practice that worked for her, she pursued a certification in teaching an embodied positive psychology practice called Let Your Yoga Dance, which combines the movement and spirituality of yoga with the sheer fun of dancing to music.

Ellen's friend Wendy, setting an intention to be less self-critical and judgmental, decided to challenge herself to a daily practice of coloring mandalas. In addition to becoming happier overall, an unintended positive consequence of her mandala-coloring routine was to unleash her creativity: She wrote a series of poems, which she ended up publishing in a book that was illustrated with her colorings!

We believe that both Ellen's and Wendy's 30-day challenges also served as moving meditation practices that, combined with other self-cultivation, increased their overall sense of well-being and opened them up to greater compassion toward others.

Step 3: Adopt a playful spirit.
Many teachers don't give themselves permission to play enough. As you begin cultivating self-compassion practices, resist the temptation to become rigid and rule-bound. Mess around. Change things up, and remain open to the unexpected. Indulge yourself. Enjoy. After all, in his book *Play: How it Shapes the Brain, Opens the Imagination, and Invigorates the Soul*, Dr. Stuart Brown's work tells us that play is healthy for our mind, body, and spirit at every age—from birth to old age!

Step 4: Commit to what works.
When you find rituals that work for you, commit to them only until you find they don't work for you anymore. Then choose something else and iterate. You may want to consider finding a friend to check in with to help you stay on track. Keeping a journal of your practices and recording your experiences helps, too. For example, Ellen tried various practices, including mindfulness meditation as one of her 30-day challenges. She found that it didn't feel right to her and had trouble sticking to a daily meditation ritual. Walking

meditation, mindful listening to music, and Let Your Yoga Dance are currently on her greatest hits list for expanding her joy and cultivating self-compassion.

◦ **OVERCOMING PUSHBACK** ◦

We hope that what we have presented in this hack is inspiring and encourages you to begin your journey to design a more compassionate life. As you improve your overall well-being, you'll likely find yourself of greater service to the students you serve. We know that change is difficult and personal and organizational transformation can sometimes feel daunting, though. That's why we have anticipated your pushback.

Great teachers are selfless. On the contrary, selflessness is the very thing that tends to lead to exhaustion, burnout, or at least bitterness or resentment for having to give out so much energy to others all day. When we don't have regular replenishing practices, and don't feel worthy of treating ourselves as we would treat a good friend, we are at greater risk for compassion fatigue. Ironically, when we turn our attention to practicing self-compassion, we become more open to helping others. Tal Ben-Shahar lectures about living a self-full life. In contrast to being selfless and being at risk of burning out from compassion fatigue, or being selfish and not caring about anyone else but yourself, being self-full is a whole being experience that prepares us to help others and make the world a better place.

I'm tough enough. Teaching is draining mentally, physically, emotionally. Ironically, being tough is often what trips us up. Acting tough, or having a hard shell, doesn't allow us to be real. When we own our vulnerabilities and at the same time recognize and work from our strengths, we open ourselves up to being compassionate toward ourselves, and in turn compassionate toward those we teach. Rather than toughening ourselves up, becoming more self-compassionate builds our resilience so we are ready to face the tough situations.

These ideas are fads. We get it. The self-help movement does feature some quackery and baseless practices. That's why we were extremely conscious of building our recommendations around science, not self-help books and snake oil salespeople. The studies we cite in our supplemental resources folders support the efficacy of our suggestions for practice, whether through quantitative laboratory experiments, qualitative field observations, interviews, grounded theory, or other data collection methods that are well-respected by the scientific community and published in peer-reviewed academic journals. Many of these practices have thousands of years of empirical evidence behind them, as they are derived from ancient wisdom traditions. And we know that the things we are recommending work, based on our own personal experiences and through hearing stories from others who are living self-compassionate lives by design.

I don't have time to practice self-compassion. We get that too. Most working people don't have time to take a course or to meditate for an hour every day. When you work in a school environment and try to balance your professional life with your personal life there are not many hours left in the day to introduce new activities or build new habits. Know that practicing self-compassion doesn't have to require a lot of time at all. For example, a good time to practice mindful breathing is when you are driving, and the traffic light turns red. In just the amount of time you are waiting for it to turn green, you can take three long, slow, deep breaths in and out, notice your inhalation and exhalation, and even silently repeat a self-compassion mantra or calming phrase with each of your breaths. If you commit to doing this at least once every day, you now have a mindful self-compassion practice that not only works to lower your stress in the moment, but also is part of your journey toward personal transformation.

Denise Carr is a high school teacher. A few years ago, when her district implemented some major changes in how students were assigned to classrooms, she almost left teaching. "None of us were having the experience I thought we should have," she shared. Frustrated with how many challenging students she had to teach in the same classroom, she felt overwhelmed and stressed on a daily basis. She realized that in order to continue in her job, "this had to be a real lifestyle change . . . I needed to have balance." She started with running and soon realized that this was not enough to give her "the space to respond to things rather than reacting to things." She decided to add yoga and meditation to her daily practice along with the running, for what she calls her "trifecta." For Denise, "movement and stillness" were the keys to her calm.

Image 1.2: **Yoga enables Denise Carr to practice self-compassion and sustain her energy for teaching.**

Denise dove deeper into her yoga practice and began teaching it in the community and at her school. She even started a yoga club for students and staff. Her own students ask her about her yoga practice and what it's all about. She's demonstrated to them how taking a breath helps her calm down and they see the positive effects of her transformation first hand.

What Denise did was to design her life around self-compassion. She acknowledged that she was frustrated and overwhelmed and knew that if she didn't change her lifestyle she would have no other choice than to leave teaching—or lose her job for not being up to the task. She recognized that she needed something that would help her, tested what it would be like to integrate movement into her life, realized that she needed even more, then added yoga, and then meditation, and then began sharing her gifts with others by teaching yoga. Denise also shared with us that she finds her mindful breathing practice to be of great help to her in particularly stressful classroom moments, and she openly demonstrates and models it for her students, with great benefits for all of them.

Running, yoga, and meditation may not be your "trifecta." But we all need to cultivate self-compassion and build lives that honor our own needs, strengths, passions, and whole-being wellness. Denise does not consider herself the "gold standard" for self-compassion, but we can follow her example of how she designed and continues to develop and refine the self-compassionate life that works for her.

Kelly Fildes Murphy has been teaching sixth-grade reading for 20 years. A few years ago, she noticed that many of her students were exhibiting increasingly notable signs of anxiety. Parents were coming in to meet with her at parent teacher conferences and telling her stories about their kids having a hard time coming to school— in some cases even needing to have the school send people to help them get out of the house. The conversation about anxious kids became prevalent in the community, and the school counselors were confirming the parents' reports and echoing their concern.

Kelly asked herself what she may be doing to contribute to her kids' anxiety. Rather than blaming herself or beating herself up, she practiced self-compassion. She immediately asked herself how she could help. "What can I do inside my classroom?" She began speaking to friends of hers in different communities and doing some research. That's when she came across mindfulness. Recognizing that she tended toward anxiety herself, she started experimenting with mindfulness in her own life. She went to a conference on mindfulness, listened to the experts, and had an "aha moment." She realized that if she could teach kids at age 11 how to handle their anxiety, they would be equipped to handle it when they were her age.

She reached out to a professor at her local college who teaches college students mindfulness and asked for help. "If I were you, I would just start it!" was the advice from this professor. So Kelly found a phone app of a singing bowl tone and began using it in her classroom. At the beginning of every class she offers a "Mindful Minute" exercise: She plays the singing bowl tone on the app and they listen to it until they can't hear it anymore. About once a week, she teaches her students a new breathing technique. From time to time she does mindful walks with them outside. "I tell them that some of these things they may choose not to use or won't appeal to them, but they'll have a menu of things to choose from in the future."

Kelly asks her students to consider how many times during the day they are asked to take a "brain break." She tells them that we all need these breaks and admits that she often has to read and reread things several times. "Mindfulness," Kelly explains, "helps us become better able to focus and not worry about other things." That eases them into a realization that perhaps they're not the only ones who get anxious and distracted. "I'm not an expert," Kelly tells her students, "but I can tell you how mindfulness helps me be less anxious and more focused." She compares building our brain muscle by practicing mindfulness to building our muscles in the gym, and helps them relate what they know about the brain to how they feel and function in their own lives. By showing them pictures of the regions of the brain—the prefrontal cortex, the hippocampus—she is able to explain how "the amygdala is like a barking dog," and asks them to notice how their brain is connected to how their body feels when they get stressed or anxious. As she introduces mindfulness practices, Kelly invites them to read more about mindfulness and to journal about how mindfulness is helping them to control their feelings of anxiety.

"There are curriculums out there, but if you practice mindfulness in your own life, then you can relate it to the kids," Kelly remarks. "They feel so much better knowing that there are other people who have the same feelings of anxiety that they do. I'm not an expert in this . . . but the more personal we make it, the better it is."

Kelly has received positive feedback from parents about how introducing mindfulness to her students has helped them be less anxious at home. Her students have told her how they have even taught their parents some of the mindfulness techniques they learned in her classroom, to ease their own stress. Kelly's principal has observed what she does with her students and supports her in continuing to integrate mindfulness in her classroom. She hopes to do staff development and a parent forum at her school to share what she has learned with others so that they can practice it and teach it to their kids.

This is how school culture is transformed. One classroom at a time. Listening and responding to what students need. With empathy and compassion.

Image 1.3: **Students in Kelly Fildes Murphy's class practice mindfulness.**

We're aware of how ethereal these recommendations may be. In fact, we hesitated to write a book about creating compassionate classrooms because we know how high-minded these conversations often are. We also know how frustrating it is to have our concerns about something elevated in the absence of potential solutions and the tools to implement them. That's what the supplemental resources folders are for. If you scan the image below or follow this link, you'll find references to the work of researchers we respect as well as a variety of tools and resources that will help you make these ideas actionable.

Here are some of the things you will find in the supplemental resources folder for Hack 1. We intend to supplement these evergreen folders over time, as our own thinking and learning evolves:

- More about the SPIRE model and how you can apply it
- References from thought leaders on compassion and positive psychology
- Practice meditations, mindfulness activities, journaling exercises, and instructional videos to support you
- A peek into Kristin Neff's research and work

Supplemental resources for Hack 1

HACK 2

SEEK DIVERSE PERSPECTIVES

Becoming Other-Centered

It's not what you look at that matters, it's what you see.
—HENRY DAVID THOREAU, AMERICAN AUTHOR

○ THE PROBLEM: SORTING PEOPLE, RATHER THAN SEEING THEM ○

Sorting helps us complete tasks quickly and efficiently. We sort socks before we pair them, our mail before we open it, and our groceries, as we unpack and put them away.

Sorting also helps us make sense of things. Clustering and categorizing ideas and information helps us synthesize, question, and determine what more we might need to know.

When we're given too much to take care of and few resources to do it with, sorting becomes a survival skill, too. We sort tasks in order to prioritize them and crises according to their potential outcomes, in order to plan our best response.

Teachers are trained to sort their students according to their needs and interests and abilities, for all of these reasons and many more. The problem is that sorting our students often prevents us from truly seeing them.

Even as we embrace promising practices like differentiated instruction and flexible grouping, our efforts often perpetuate a kind of sorting that perpetuates division. This is particularly problematic when students are consistently grouped according to their perceived needs rather than their strengths or interests.

Perception is everything, and often ours is limited.

Compassion calls us to see one another in all of our complexities.

How might we widen and deepen our view? How might we look at one another closely? Longer? How might we lean in and listen hard to the stories they have to share?

When teachers define the limits of their own understanding and demonstrate how they are working to overcome them, they model important values and behaviors for their students.

◦ THE HACK: KNOWING THAT WE JUST DON'T KNOW ◦

If we're to build compassionate classrooms, we might begin by helping students understand, appreciate, and seek diversity. It's not enough to simply tolerate those who are different from us. It's not enough merely accept them, either. These may appear to be noble efforts, but in practice, they often illuminate our differences just enough to divide us. Teachers who commit to cultivating compassion establish contexts that make seeking diversity a key driver of successful thinking, learning, and work. They illuminate the consequences of homogeneity, and they empower students to better understand how diversity works inside of their small and larger worlds.

More importantly, they position themselves as learners.

We're all confined by our own experiences and identities. Even as the boundaries established by race, gender, ethnicity, socio-economics, physical and mental abilities and sexual orientation begin to intersect and blend, it's important to recognize how our unique personal experiences shape and even limit our perspectives. There is no shame in this.

In our ever-changing world, it's difficult to know what we don't know about those who are different from us and all too easy to oversimplify that which is incredibly complex. When teachers define the limits of their own understanding and demonstrate how they are working to overcome them, they model important values and behaviors for their students.

Much has been said about the importance of valuing diversity. How might we model processes by which people genuinely achieve this, though? There is something to be said for knowing that we just don't know and helping students position themselves as learners when they find themselves in similar positions. The strategies that follow will support you.

◦ WHAT YOU CAN DO TOMORROW ◦

Grounding these lofty ideas in a concrete reality requires specific action. Each of the steps below are easy enough to take tomorrow, but worthy of sustained implementation. Where might you begin? Start your planning here, and explore the supplemental resources folder at the end of this hack to deepen your learning and gain more support.

- **EMPATHY MAP IN ORDER TO APPRECIATE COMPLEXITIES.** An empathy map is a tool that helps students and teachers gain a better understanding of one another in just one class period. As users engage with it, they put themselves in another's shoes, developing interpretations of how those people feel, what they see, what they hear, what they say, and what they do in specific contexts. Ideas are typically shared on sticky notes or index cards, as users move from one dimension of the map to another, projecting themselves into the characters they wish to understand better, in order to empathize with them. You will find examples of empathy maps, protocols for using them, and printable posters and charts in the supplemental resources folder for this hack.

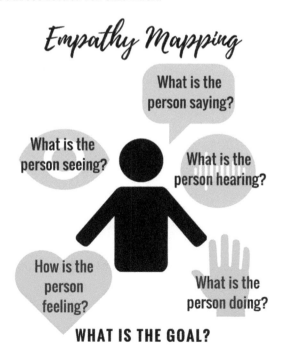

Image 2.1: Empathy Mapping to Deepen Our Understanding of Classmates

- **ILLUMINATE DIVERSITY IN YOUR OWN CLASSROOM.** Create opportunities for students to deepen their self-awareness and consider the complexities of their experiences and character. Use these discoveries to enrich perspective-taking during problem seeking and solving sessions. Demonstrate, on a daily basis, how diversity elevates your thinking, learning, and work. Human Affinity Mapping is a powerful protocol that illuminates intersectionalities in groups of all kinds, including classroom communities. You'll find it in the supplemental resources folder for this hack.

- **DIVERSIFY AND HUMANIZE YOUR DATA.** Our test-obsessed culture places an emphasis on quantitative data that is all too appealing. Numbers breed a kind of false confidence that inspires quick conclusions and sorting rather than seeing. Qualitative approaches, including those embraced by design thinkers, help us take a more human approach. They allow us to diversify our data in ways that enable us to see others better.

    Immersion is a powerful way to begin. Rather than merely inviting students to bring their lives into your classroom, commit to leaving it as well. Shadow your students each day for just a few moments outside of your classroom. Get a sense of their experiences in the cafeteria, in the hall between classes, at their practices, or in another teacher's room. Ask yourself what you might not know about them collectively and especially as individuals. Consider which of their daily experiences might be the most revealing, and try to show up for them tomorrow. Devote a few moments of each day to immersing yourself in even one student's wider world. The next day, pick another. Reflect on what you're learning. What perspectives have you gained?

Coach your students to practice immersion as well, even in the confines of your own classroom, school, and community. Who do they need to understand better? How might they enter their world? How can you help them see what matters? What's present? What's missing?

Approximate situations that don't allow for immersion or replication. Angela remembers facilitating a writing workshop with high school students who were eager to write about some of the complex problems challenging their own community. When a 15-year-old boy raised his hand to suggest that he wanted to better understand heroin addiction without entering the unsafe world of heroin addicts, a powerful brainstorming session ensued. "You could try to find stories written by addicts," another writer suggested, and this seemed like a viable option. Much can be learned from those who use their words to share their experiences. Stories allow us to enter worlds unlike our own—even those that are distant or dangerous. They help us practice empathy when true immersion is too risky, too costly, or otherwise unrealistic.

Observation deepens our understanding of complex people and situations. Begin by defining what you hope to learn, and then decide how you might learn it through careful observation. When Ellen was interested in learning more about why a student was being disruptive in one of Angela's writing workshops, she assumed a curious posture and began documenting exactly what the child was doing and when she was doing it. Rather than reacting, she suspended judgment long enough to practice empathy through observation. This revealed an unexpected root cause for the child's behavior, inspiring a far more effective response.

Interviews add important context and complexity to our observations, too. Ask broad questions of those you hope to understand better before posing ones that are far more pointed. Record exactly what your subjects say, not only what you hear, and whenever possible, invite them to share stories, analogies, and metaphors that reveal important context and nuance.

Challenge your students to use interviews to their advantage as well, particularly when they find someone or something confusing, uncomfortable, or even offensive. Model the process yourself, and demonstrate how the discoveries you made through interviewing inspired better choices and decision making.

- **COACH COMPASSIONATE LISTENING.** Aruni Nan Futuronsky, a faculty member at the Kripalu Center for Yoga and Health, invites us to engage in co-listening: a practice that engenders conscious communication by creating space for speakers and listeners to have clear, deep, and connected conversations. The exchange begins with an agreement; the listener serves as a silent and supportive witness while the speaker expresses thoughts, feelings, and ideas for three minutes. Then, when the time has expired, roles are reversed. Rounds may be repeated multiple times, until both speaker and listener feel heard. Committing to silent but supportive listening, speaking at length without fear of interruption, and ensuring equitable time within each round motivate us to remain present, suspend judgment, and express ourselves fully. Compassionate listening can be especially powerful when people disagree and especially when their diverse perspectives create conflict. Sometimes, having permission to not react or repair what we think might be broken in another person's reasoning is all that we need to stop sorting and, instead, start hearing and seeing people in all of their complexities. As Dr. Brené Brown, research professor at the University of Houston Graduate School of Social Work, suggests, it's harder to hate people close up.

○ A BLUEPRINT FOR FULL IMPLEMENTATION ○

Compassion thrives inside of systems that commit to it with great intention. We believe that real change begins at the classroom level, but we also know that sustaining it requires everyone inside of a system to learn the language of compassion and practice it with intention. Here's how school leaders can make that happen.

Step 1: Seek diverse perspectives at every level of your system. When might you use empathy mapping to better understand your colleagues, leaders, or those you lead? How could co-listening slow your reaction time long enough to get a better sense of who people are, what they need, and what they might be able to contribute to your solution-seeking processes? What specific steps will you take to make diverse perspective-taking a systemic norm? You'll find further reading, reflection tools, and catalysts for action planning inside of the supplemental resources folder for this hack.

Step 2: Expand and then assess the use of ethnographic strategies.
Ethnography by definition is a portrait of people. It's a social science research method that relies heavily on participatory experiences, including those mentioned earlier in this hack: immersion, approximation, observation, and interview. When we practice ethnography in the field of education, we embrace the fact that human beings, in all of their imperfections, provide a level of meaning that sterile quantitative research and methods cannot.

How might you begin to gather, analyze, and better value the findings that emerge from this kind of research? Consider walking the halls of your school and taking note of your observations. What do the displays reveal about people's values or, at the very least, the alignment between their values and their display choices?

Rather than simply analyzing documents, photographs, and videos, ask yourself: Who captured this evidence? When? Why? Most importantly, what does each artifact reveal about the values and perspectives of the person who captured it? Which other stories or perspectives are missing? How might you access them?

Consider making a study of body movements and motion. Body language often reveals withheld or even unconscious thoughts. How people take up space and moderate the distance they place between themselves and others is meaningful as well. These data can help us analyze situations with greater accuracy, particularly when we remain aware of the challenges and potential drawbacks inherent in their use. You may learn more about ethnographic research by visiting the supplemental resources folder for this hack.

Step 3: Engage community liaisons and cultural brokers.
Community liaisons are trusted individuals who have deep knowledge of a person or community and a willingness to advocate for their interests and needs. Liaisons help us seek diverse perspectives when those we are eager to serve are unable or even unwilling to engage with us directly. Cultural brokers are much like community liaisons, but they also have deep wisdom of a cultural community's values, beliefs, and practices. Community liaisons and cultural brokers help those outside of their diverse systems gain a deeper awareness of the most culturally appropriate ways to serve them.

Which cultural communities comprise your school system? Who are the best liaisons for those communities, and how might you better engage them? How might their perspectives inform the way you gather and interpret critical data? How might they help you develop greater cultural competence? You will find a guidance document that can help you plan your work with liaisons and develop greater cultural sensitivity by visiting the supplemental resources folder for this hack.

Step 4: Establish feedback loops.
Feedback loops have the potential to strengthen and sustain the connection between what we're learning about one another and how we're behaving and teaching in response. The premise is fairly simple—when people receive timely feedback about their actions and incentives to improve them, everyone continues to make better choices that improve school culture.

Feedback loops are built in four stages: First, we gather evidence about specific behaviors. Then, we share that data in a way that resonates with individuals. Next, we clear pathways toward a better land. Finally, we offer company and sustained support as individuals begin their journey toward improvement.

How might you establish feedback loops that improve school culture? Which loops might help students, teachers, and leaders practice empathy? Which could improve cultural competence?

○ OVERCOMING PUSHBACK ○

Seeking diversity requires us to explore our own identities, seek out those who will illuminate our biases, and sit with discomfort. This is challenging—even unsettling—work, and as we sink into it, thoughts like these often rise to the surface.

I'm already a tolerant teacher. When we began planning and drafting this book, we did so with a deep awareness of our own capacity for tolerance and the knowledge that despite our best efforts, we still did not know all that we could know about embracing and elevating diversity. We've learned that the difference between tolerance and acceptance can be substantial and that in order to transform school culture we must not only seek and appreciate diversity, but situate it as the gateway to reaching our fullest potential as a community of learners and teachers.

We're often unaware of the casual and even unintended ways we dismiss, discredit, and denigrate those who are socially marginalized. The term microaggression was coined by Harvard University Professor Chester M. Pierce in 1970. Pierce wanted to define the kind of subtle insults he witnessed non-black Americans inflicting on black Americans. His work inspired others to begin noticing and naming the microaggressions imposed on other marginalized groups, including women, members of the LGBTQ community, people coping with mental illness, those with atypical physical or intellectual abilities, and the elderly.

While some argue that the concept of microaggression is not well-substantiated by research and that promoting it may have the potential to perpetuate victimhood culture, developing an awareness of common microaggressions deepens our capacity for empathy and encourages us to consider diverse perspectives. It also helps us make more informed observations and ask better questions of ourselves and of others, too.

How might we help our students notice potential microaggressions without perpetuating shame or a sense of victimhood? Considering this question is worthy work. You'll find more information about microaggression, including tools for classroom use, in the supplemental resources folder for this hack.

When you over-empathize with one group, you infringe on another. So, how might we ensure the right balance? So much of what we do to create compassionate classrooms requires critical thinking, experimentation, and problem seeking and solving. It's quite possible to get this wrong. What's important is that we do more than merely intend to do right. We must create the space to make that happen. How might you check in with different groups in order to take their temperature? What might you learn by inviting students to think and speak about intersectionality? How might reflection inform our perspectives and practices as we work to improve classroom and school culture?

Too many of my colleagues maintain strong biases and stereotypes. Roshi Joan Halifax is a priest in the Japanese Zen religion. One of her most powerful core messages, "Strong back, soft front," invites all of us to consider the relationship between equanimity, or self-possession, and compassion.

How might we uphold ourselves and create compassionate classrooms and schools with integrity while remaining open to people and situations just as they are? How should we respond when our colleagues reveal biases or practice stereotyping in ways that disappoint or even anger us? When we find ourselves in these situations, we ask: How might we lean in and listen hard, in order to understand them better?

Researcher and author Brené Brown suggests that people are harder to hate up close. She suggests that we engage those who are different from us, opening conversations about our diverse perspectives, and paying attention to our discomfort. As it mounts, we need to stop ourselves from disengaging and instead lean in and listen harder. We might ask, "Can you say more about that?" We might practice compassionate listening as well. Then we might respectfully challenge the biases and stereotypes that are revealed. We might own our own, as well.

Such exchanges aren't always in anyone's best interests, though. When people make denigrating or dehumanizing statements, our response must be very different. Brown reminds us that the traumatized are not responsible for transforming perpetrators. As teachers, we need to be aware of the signals that suggest that leaning in, listening hard, and evolving together simply isn't possible. Sometimes, we're responsible for disrupting stereotypes, protesting injustice, and taking brave steps to prevent further harm.

◦ THE HACK IN ACTION ◦

Larry Schwarz, a high school teacher in the Miami-Dade County Public School system, doesn't merely tolerate complexity and diversity—he appreciates it. This enables him to engage students whose challenging life experiences often make school seem like an irrelevant distraction.

"Many of my students believe that they will be in prison or even dead before their twenty-fifth birthdays," he explains. "They've grown up marginalized in many ways, and they have little hope that they will be able to live a life that is any different from those who have come before them."

He knows this because he's spoken with his students about their struggles and their ambitions. He accepts them as they are, and he maintains a position of curiosity rather than judgment about the choices they make.

"I always present options, based on my observations and the things I learn about their lives outside of my classroom," he continues. He also invites his students to empathize with him when he sets boundaries that they aren't comfortable with. "I'll ask a kid who struggles to make good choices when left unsupervised to tell me what he would do in my position, if he or she were me. 'If I give you this opportunity to use a hall pass without my supervision, what do you suppose I might worry about?'" Larry tells me his students make honest assessments and that his willingness to be honest about his concerns without shaming them deepens their trust.

"I'm willing to make myself vulnerable with them, too. I'll speak openly about my struggles with my weight or other issues that can be shame-inducing. I never diminish or disrespect myself. I don't beat myself up. I try to show them that I trust them, and I also model what it looks like to practice self-respect even as I deal with my own perceived imperfections." This helps Larry's students see him as a complex person as well.

Larry relies on historical figures and literary characters to deepen his students' capacity for empathy as well. Rather than making a purely academic study of their place in time or function inside of a narrative, he poses questions that help students consider the challenges they faced. He helps students humanize the people they find within the pages of their textbooks and novels. He inspires them to turn to these figures for inspiration, validation, and perspective-taking. People aren't always right or wrong, and neither are the decisions they make.

Except when people choose to marginalize others.

Alberto M. Carvalho, superintendent of Miami-Dade County Public Schools, understands the need to take specific actions in order to better understand his students' needs. He advocates for compassionate listening, meeting with transgender students, their parents, school counselors, and administrators to determine appropriate school bathroom use on a case-by-case basis. This practice has been in place for many years at Miami-Dade County Public Schools, which provides gender neutral bathrooms for all students, and when the Trump administration announced an end to federal protections for transgender youth, he took a strong public stand on their behalf, assuring all that they were still protected under the district's anti-discrimination policies.

Image 2.2: Miami-Dade County Public Schools Superintendent Alberto M. Carvalho makes compassion a public practice.

"We will not allow any of our students to be pushed back into the dark corner of fear, intimidation, or discrimination," he said in a tweet. This is a perfect example of recognizing when the best course of action is resistance and advocacy.

In our work, we've noticed that one of the most powerful things about perspective-taking is its potential to relieve teachers of their need to have all of the answers. In fact, when we plan to seek diverse perspectives with intention, we make a deep commitment to curiosity rather than certainty. We also begin adopting far more agile tools and practices. Rather than assuming who our students are and what they might need, we listen to them, in order to learn. Rather than pre-planning to control every detail of our lessons and the learning outcomes they target, we ask ourselves how we might engage our students in more collaborative curriculum design processes.

Finally, and perhaps most importantly, we begin to dedicate at least as much time to envisioning the kind of people we would like our curriculum to produce as we do defining learning targets that attend to the content and skills of our academic domains. In our experiences, teachers never minimize the need to shape their classroom cultures with intention. They often lack explicit tools for doing so, though. You'll find some useful ones in the supplemental resources folder for this hack, including:

- Examples of empathy maps, protocols, and printable posters for classroom and system-wide use
- Human affinity mapping protocols
- Tools for making the most of immersion, observation, and approximation
- References to the research and work of Brené Brown and Roshi Joan Halifax

Supplemental resources for Hack 2

CRAFT YOUR CLASSROOM CULTURE

Shaping Attitudes, Values, Beliefs, and Behaviors

Schools could, without compromising either, teach both the skills of well-being and the skills of achievement.
—MARTIN E.P. SELIGMAN, PHD, AUTHOR, EDUCATOR, POSITIVE PSYCHOLOGIST

◦ THE PROBLEM: NOT KNOWING WHERE OR HOW TO START ◦

A teacher recently told Ellen that after many years of reporting to the same administration, the district assigned her school a new building principal. Not knowing who this person was, or anything about him, she attended a school-wide meeting where she was taken aback by the first thing he asked: "How are the children?" She said that at first everyone looked quizzically at him and murmured, "Fine?" Then he explained that instead of saying "How do you do?" when they meet people, the Masai of Kenya customarily greet each other with "Kasserian Ingera?" which means "How are the children?" to which they hope for the response "All the children are well." The principal further explained that in Masai society, when all the children are well, that is an indicator of the present—and future—health and well-being of their society. Knowing that this was her new leader's perspective, the teacher said she felt hopeful. Rather than coming into the school ready to transform its culture, he entered it eager to assess it, and he saw the wellness of the children as an important indicator of health. He's not alone.

In our conversations with teachers and school leaders, they tell us that they see a need to shift their school culture to a more positive one. They know that paying attention to the social and emotional needs of their students is essential in creating an atmosphere of safety that sets the stage for real learning. They've seen the power of listening to their students, responding positively to their efforts to succeed, and showing them that they believe in them and in their capabilities. They recognize that getting to know their students and what they are interested in can be motivating and is an opportunity to build relationships. They know all of this in their hearts, yet they are not sure how to translate it into actionable steps toward positive school transformation.

The notion of transforming school culture is by nature an ethereal concept and a seemingly daunting mission. What is a positive school culture? How do we measure it? How do we know when it's transformed? Who is responsible for transforming my school's culture? What is my role as a teacher?

You are probably asking yourself where transforming your classroom falls within the increasing demands of your life. You also may be wondering how to situate this work beside the content you are charged with delivering, and skills you are responsible for teaching inside your classroom. And you may be concerned about the uncertainty of how your students, parents, colleagues, and school leaders will respond to your efforts to create a compassionate classroom.

Crafting a compassionate classroom may feel like a herculean task, too large for any one teacher to take on. But, just like your own personal transformation, systemic change must be broken down into manageable steps. And the bottom line is: You have to start somewhere! And your own classroom is the perfect place to start.

◦ THE HACK: ACT AS IF . . . ◦

We believe that the best way to create a compassionate classroom is to act as if it already were. That means behaving compassionately toward yourself and in turn demonstrating to your students how they should behave, using your actions as a model. It also means bringing positive, hopeful energy to the classroom so that you set the stage for making positive interactions the norm. By showing students that you care about them and that you believe in their capacity to act respectfully and kindly toward you and their classmates, you will be elevating their expectations for their behavior—and your expectations for their potential. If you act as if all members of your classroom are deserving of respect, you will engender an atmosphere of open-heartedness, kindness, appreciation, and authentic connection. Those are the basic components of compassion. And we all have the potential to embody this.

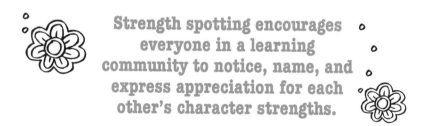

Strength spotting encourages everyone in a learning community to notice, name, and express appreciation for each other's character strengths.

Researchers at the VIA (Values in Action) Institute on Character have developed a framework for assessing character strengths. It is built on the premise that what we all have in common—across gender, culture, religion, ethnicity, place of origin—is a personal collection of 24 character strengths. While each of us has certain dominant strengths, known as "signature strengths," we have the capability of acting on and developing any of the 24 character traits at any time. Using the VIA strengths in the classroom provides a way to recognize or "spot" one another's strengths—for students and teachers alike—and an opportunity to galvanize groups and incentivize behavior modification without resorting to the use of punishment or rewards. Rather than relying on behavior charts and goal setting that is driven by the desire to fix what is broken, the character strengths help us understand how the virtues we share in common along with our differences make us stronger. Strength spotting encourages everyone in a learning community to notice, name, and express appreciation for each other's character strengths.

The VIA strengths framework can serve as a vehicle for acting "as if" your classroom were built on empathy and compassion. Seeing and appreciating the positive contributions that we all make to our classroom community by expressing our character strengths through our attitudes, values, beliefs and behaviors is the foundation that can scaffold the transformation of your classroom.

○ WHAT YOU CAN DO TOMORROW ○

Here are some concrete actions you can implement immediately to begin the process of crafting your classroom community built around strengths, appreciating the good, and noticing what's working as you go.

- **JUST BEGIN.** Don't wait to feel like you have a perfect plan. Just begin with empathy and curiosity and allow yourself to grow as you go. You don't have to know your outcome. You just have to begin with understanding the general direction of where you want to go and have a vision for what you want to create and figure it out along the way.

- **DEFINE YOUR PRINCIPLES.** Empower your students by engaging them in the process of defining what a compassionate classroom looks like while offering your own ideas. Talk about what it means to act with kindness and respect toward one another. What does it mean to value everyone's contributions, expertise, and points of view? How can you value each other's strengths? What do you expect from one another as you interact as a group? What are your beliefs about your students and your students' classmates and their potential for behaving compassionately? What classroom guidelines for behavior can you agree on that represent these principles? How should they be expressed? How should they be encouraged? Are you seeing each other rather than sorting? Angela and Ellen went through a similar exercise, defining their principles about school culture and compassionate classrooms when they began writing this book. (See Image I.1 Our 10 Principles.)

- **ASSESS YOUR CURRENT REALITY.** Examine your own classroom and assess how your principles are aligning with what you see happening in your classroom. What components of compassion that you defined are apparent? To what degree are they operating on a daily basis? Which principles need strengthening through action? How are you modeling empathy and self-compassion for your students? How are you encouraging curiosity and creativity among your students? To what extent are you facilitating multidisciplinary thinking, initiative, and teamwork? Use the compassionate classroom assessment tool that we have developed for you, which can be found in the supplemental resources folder for Hack 3.

- **UNIFY AROUND STRENGTHS.** Learn more about the VIA strengths and brainstorm how you may be able to integrate them into your classroom. Don't worry about coming up with any special activities or classroom exercises at first. Just begin to think about shifting your focus from identifying and remediating deficits in your students and yourself to recognizing and appreciating character strengths and how they show themselves in the classroom. Begin strength-spotting your students using the VIA character strengths, and integrate character strengths language into daily classroom conversation. It's not about false praise, but encouragement that's grounded in reality. If you're ready to begin strength spotting with your students, visit the supplemental resources folder for this hack. You'll find activities to support this work there, as well as a peek into the process that we used in New York State during a visit to Chappaqua Central School District.

Image 3.1: **Students at Angela's Make Writing Pop Up Studio in Chappaqua indentifying each other's top VIA character strengths.**

- **FOCUS ON WHAT'S WORKING.** Because of our need to survive, our brains are hardwired to notice danger, threat, and negative emotions more than situations of safety, comfort, and pleasurable emotions. Not that we don't notice the good in our lives, but we need to put more effort into focusing our attention on the things we appreciate and the people who bring us joy. The most accomplished people ask themselves what's working and build on their successes. When you focus on the good, you and your students will experience positive emotions such as joy, excitement and pride. They will feel more motivated to learn and will be more engaged in the learning process. Positivity researcher and author Barbara Fredrickson, PhD, has observed a phenomenon she calls "positivity resonance" where positive emotions "broaden and build" on each other. That's how you create and sustain a positive classroom culture. As Tal Ben-Shahar says, "When you appreciate the good, the good will appreciate."

⚬ A BLUEPRINT FOR FULL IMPLEMENTATION ⚬

Bill Burnett and Dave Evans, Stanford University's design educators and authors of *Designing Your Life: How to Build a Well-Lived Joyful Life*, teach their students how to use the design process to build lives that are meaningful, joyful and fulfilling. This work precedes systemic change, preparing us to serve as a beacon for others. Here are a few steps that you might take to begin moving the compassion that is built in your classrooms into the hallways and throughout the school.

Step 1: Get curious and imagine.

After you've defined your vision with your students about what your compassionate classroom can look like, begin imagining what your school culture would look like if it were built upon empathy and compassion. Although you can only control your own actions and cultivate your own self-compassion, remember that the work you do in your classroom and the tone you set will undoubtedly seep into the rest of your school community. After all, your students interact with other teachers, school leaders, and parents. Students can serve as ambassadors of compassion by bringing the practices, attitudes, values and beliefs about how to act toward one another into their homes and elsewhere. The social emotional lessons you teach by example can serve as a basis for positive transformation. Challenge your students to imagine and then define the outcomes that they could work toward as they try to move their entire school toward compassion.

Kristal Hickmon is a retired school principal and district administrator in Miami, Florida, who made establishing a compassionate school culture her priority. Ellen's son will always remember how Kristal made it a point of greeting her students at the door as they entered their middle school building each morning. With a smile, direct eye contact and a positive comment (or gentle correction), Kristal welcomed each of them, by name. On the morning announcements, her inspiring and motivational message to the entire school, including the teachers and staff, was "Make it a great day . . . or not . . . the choice is yours."

Step 2: Try out possibilities.

Just as you are on a journey to expand your open-heartedness by exploring new practices and building positive habits, there is a world of practical possibilities that can help you transform the spirit of your school. For example, there are multiple ways you can introduce strengths-spotting and the language of character strengths to your administrators, colleagues, and other staff members. Shifting your classroom focus to spotting students' strengths and recognizing how they put them into action has the power to have a ripple effect in changing beliefs and attitudes about students and their potential system-wide. Take a peek at the Strengths Spotting Center that we left for you in the supplemental resources folder at the end of this hack. How might you use it in your classroom? How could it be used system-wide?

Step 3: Observe, reflect, and assess what's working.

Monitor your progress by keeping a journal of observations and notable moments. You may want to make it a daily habit of writing down three good things that moved your school closer to compassion and reflect on how they may relate to positive changes you've been creating. You also may want to keep a "Compassionate Classroom Journal" to jot down your reflections and document your journey. Invite students to contribute to it, too. In the supplemental resources folder for this hack, we have provided you with a printable template for journaling about your compassionate classroom, with guided questions to assist you in appreciating your experiences.

Step 4: Prepare to weather storms.
Expect setbacks and obstacles. But regardless of the challenges that will inevitably come up, try to reframe them as opportunities for growth. Keep your focus on what's working and build on that. Research in the area of organizational change has shown that when consultants come into a company to help them solve a problem, the most successful approach is to identify and appreciate what has gone right in that organization and use lessons from those experiences. Sometimes it's difficult to find the positive, but it's always worth looking for. Ask yourself: How might you address the challenge? Do you need to change your plan? Adjust your expectations? Iterate on it. Hacking school culture is an ongoing process. You are finding your way toward a compassionate classroom that can influence your entire school culture.

○ OVERCOMING PUSHBACK ○

We know that there will be people who think that school culture can be created or changed only from the top down. They will be skeptical that you can have influence and discourage you from even trying. You will even doubt yourself and think "Who am I to dare to take on this mission?" We all feel like small fish in big ponds when we work in systems. And we know that we often feel like we are swimming upstream, especially when we have to defend ourselves for doing what we know is right in our hearts. Here are some ways to push back against the doubters, including our own skeptical selves.

Acting "as if" makes me feel like an imposter. We know that it's uncomfortable to pretend to feel, believe, or act some way when you have a strong value for being authentic. But this is not about pretending. There is solid research that shows that lasting change in behavior, attitudes, and beliefs starts with action. In fact, studies show that smiling can make us feel happier, power posing can make us feel more confident, and nodding when listening to someone increases our likelihood of agreeing with them. So, act compassionately with intention and see what happens.

I'm daunted and discouraged by the distance between our current reality and our ultimate vision. That's okay. Remember that taking small steps in the right direction is how you create transformation. As long as you have a clear idea of where you are going, you are trying things out, testing, iterating, and have designed your transformation from a place of empathy, you are making great progress. Ellen's teacher Tal reminds us all that at every moment we have a choice. Those moments add up to a lifetime, and our choices add up to a life.

We don't have the time to work toward systemic change. Remember that this is an ongoing process. Transformation takes time, but every step you take is progress toward finding your way. By creating a compassionate culture in your classroom you are influencing systemic change at your school even if it's not obvious. We believe that the greatest, most lasting change comes from the ground up.

I'm the only teacher who cares about this. If you scratch the surface, this is probably not true. But, assuming it is, we invite you to embrace being a brave change-maker for the good of your students and for your school. Looking at the big picture, you are not alone. If you do find other teachers at your school or elsewhere who care about crafting compassionate classrooms, then share ideas, observations, and successes, and support each other! We are all in this together.

When special education teacher Kathy Rowland greeted Angela and Ellen on the first day of the intensive writing program they were hosting for the students in her school, she did so with a fair amount of trepidation. She knew many of the kids well, and some of them were challenging to work with. She knew that she would have to be proactive if the week was going to be a success.

"Some teachers are really overwhelmed by him," she smiled, and Angela turned to her with interest. While other children were settling into their rhythm as writers, one young man was out of his seat, hopping from one foot to the other, and swinging dramatically between tables. He didn't want to sit. He didn't want to write. He wanted to move, and it was distracting everyone else. Sitting still was a consistent classroom norm, after all. "He's an interesting kid," Kathy reflected aloud. "He's quick. Funny."

He was also raising every teacher's blood pressure.

An agenda was set, and the learning outcomes for the day's session were clear.

Teachers were gathered to participate in a lesson study, and while it may not have been his intention, this student was throwing everyone off task. Waves of impatience rippled through the room, and Kathy and Angela were tempted to remove the student, but instead, they gave him a bucket full of blocks, foam balls, and other loose parts. They gave him his own table, and then they invited him to build.

Every few minutes, he would stop and roam the room for a bit, often swinging from tables on either side of the aisle or skipping through the open space near the window ledge. After a few moments of movement, he'd return to his table and continue tinkering with his creation. As he did, Kathy began snapping pictures of his process and the product that was emerging from it. He didn't seem to notice. He was focused on his build.

"Would you like to use these photos and the tower you're creating to tell your story?" Kathy asked, and the writer readily agreed. Moments later, a richer writing idea emerged from his work. He pulled up a stool and signed onto a laptop. He was writing. Contentedly.

Rather than attempting to control, discipline, or direct this student, Kathy helped Angela make space for his interests and deepen his awareness of his own needs. This wasn't comfortable work. It required patience, flexibility, a willingness to listen, and a great deal of daily reflection. The results were worth it, though. On the final day of writing studio, this student watched every student say their goodbyes and head out the door, and then he wandered back into the classroom with one final question and a powerful reflection.

"Can I please take some of those loose parts home to use?" he asked. "This week was really good for me."

Angela filled a bucket to the brim and handed it to him, grinning.

"Thanks," he said.

Throughout the week of the intensive writing program, Angela and Ellen introduced the VIA character strengths to the students and the teachers by integrating various activities into the curriculum to describe their fictional characters, as well as using the language of specific character strengths to raise awareness of what each student brought to the writing workshop. What was particularly notable was how this initially disruptive and continually challenging student was perceived by his peers when they were asked to characterize their own and each other's strengths. Having witnessed this student's transition from being uncomfortable with writing to focusing and immersing himself in building, they recognized his obvious creativity and chose that trait to describe his top strength. From then on, the mood shifted; he owned his creativity and the other students—and teachers—saw him that way. In just one week, working with the VIA strengths created a new way for students to look at themselves and others and to appreciate one another's gifts.

Christine Boyer, an elementary school teacher at the Heathcote School in Scarsdale, New York, has been teaching fifth grade for seventeen years. Always looking for new ways to meet the needs and interests of her students, Christine attended Angela's intensive summer writing program as an observer. It was there that she became familiar with the VIA character strengths and started generating ideas for how she could integrate the language of character into her own classroom. At the beginning of the new school year, she introduced the concept of character strengths to her students by showing them a couple of the films that were produced for Character Day by Tiffany Shlain, and using supporting materials to spur discussion. She found that her students found the films powerful, and from them they generated a number of questions to deepen their understanding of character and how the traits are revealed through our behavior.

Observing their interest, Christine posted definitions of the strengths on the classroom walls to reinforce this perspective. To make the strengths even more tangible and hands-on, her students painted rocks with each one representing a character trait. These rocks are lined up on a shelf in the classroom, and her students are free to go over and choose the strength they need when they are working out a problem, negotiating a difficult relationship, trying to describe characters in their own writing, or when they need a physical reminder of something they are trying to articulate.

Christine finds that "putting character front and center" has not only created a common language for dialogue, but has also created a "group dynamic" that's formed around strengths, where students take the time to get to know one another. She has also noticed how having the character rocks present and available to students allows them to work out their differences with one another. When two boys who were having a conflict at lunch came back to the classroom, she invited them to go over to the rocks, consider what had just happened, and pick the strengths that they each needed to work on. Christine then took the opportunity to sit down with the boys to discuss the conflict and hear their suggestions for a solution within the context of character strengths. "It was a powerful experience to see them problem solving around character, and how they could be part of the solution. They took ownership for their behavior, rather than me having to lecture them."

Other teachers in Christine's building have asked her about how they can integrate a character strengths-based approach into their classrooms. Christine shares her classroom experiences using strengths with her colleagues at informal lunch gatherings and faculty meetings, as well as communicating with a wider audience through Twitter and other social media platforms. In addition, her fifth graders have buddied with a second-grade class, and her students have introduced the concept of strengths by creating character rocks together.

Christine also is involved in a project with school administrators to create a character-strength rock garden at the school to spread a "feeling of positivity" through a "visual nudge." She would love to leave a tangible reminder behind for her school community, "a legacy that says 'Christine Boyer was here and [character] has meaning to us.'"

Image 3.2: Christine Boyer's students created tangible reminders of their character strengths to use in class when needed.

On a systemic level, the Geelong Grammar School in Australia has been a testing ground for positive education. In a project originally initiated by Martin Seligman, PhD, of the University of Pennsylvania, and the late Christopher Peterson, PhD, of the University of Michigan, in collaboration with other colleagues who have continued the research, it is an example of how an entire school culture can be built around the VIA strengths. Driven by the evidence-based guidelines to promote flourishing—social and emotional as well as academic—across the whole school community, their model for positive education includes six domains: positive engagement, positive accomplishment, positive health, positive emotions, positive relationships, and positive purpose, with character strengths interwoven throughout.

Everyone at the school, from students to teachers to support staff, is trained in the language of the VIA, and has a thorough understanding of their own signature strengths. The VIA-strengths framework is used to identify strengths in others, as well as exploring, discussing, and developing their own Values in Action on a daily basis. The researchers have found that the VIA-strengths framework helps build students' resilience and contributes to their flourishing by supporting a culture of connectedness and respect across the school community.

We would love to hear your stories about how you are crafting your compassionate classroom. Use the hashtag #compassionateclassrooms when you share on Twitter.

We have seen firsthand how a strengths-based approach can set the tone for classroom culture and, in turn, school climate. When you focus on what's working and build on that, you can create and continue to craft your classroom in ways that bring your vision to life.

If you'd like more resources to support your journey, you will find them in the supplemental resources folder for Hack 3:

- Link to the VIA Character Survey and description of strengths
- Useful articles for educators on VIA character strengths
- Classroom activities for identifying character strengths
- Strengths-Spotting Center Protocol that we created for classrooms
- Links to Character Day videos and free materials for educators
- Videos from positive psychology and positive education
- Research on positive education and link to book about the Geelong School
- Photos from Christine Boyer's fifth-grade classroom

Supplemental resources for Hack 3

HACK 4

DISTINGUISHING BLAME FROM RESPONSE ABILITY:

Building Equity

I imagine one of the reasons people cling to their hates so stubbornly is because they sense, once hate is gone, they will be forced to deal with pain.
—JAMES BALDWIN, AMERICAN AUTHOR

○ THE PROBLEM: DISCHARGING PAIN RATHER THAN DEALING WITH IT ○

If your current daily life is an exercise in the avoidance of pain, then you might want to think twice before dedicating any part of it to the field of education. Everyone knows that teaching is a tough gig, but that's not where this hack is heading. We intend to explore the notion that in order to serve students well, teachers must be strong enough to bear witness to their pain and brave enough to sit with their own, as well.

Those who lack this sort of fortitude risk more than their mental health when they enter the classroom. They risk their students' well-being, too.

Compassionate classrooms are not fueled by pity. They're places where brilliant and vulnerable humans gather to learn things without fear of losing status or the respect of those they admire. And learning is an incredibly imperfect experience.

When we expect others to accept responsibility, we pin them there until they make satisfactory amends. Responsibility is often about what happened and who needs to fix what is broken, not what we might create together.

Those who disregard, minimize, or compartmentalize pain will struggle to create compassionate classrooms. These behaviors alone create division and leave people feeling as if they don't matter. Brené Brown warns us of an even worse phenomenon, though: Given the choice between tolerating discomfort or discharging it, many human beings will often opt for the latter. When they do, they resort to blaming and shaming themselves and others.

Our classroom and school cultures are poisoned by this phenomenon.

◦ THE HACK: REFRAME RESPONSIBILITY ◦

Responsibilities are weighty matters. They're serious. Even burdensome. When we accept responsibility, we often shift our attention to the past. When we expect others to accept responsibility, we pin them there until they make satisfactory amends. Responsibility is often about what happened and who needs to fix what is broken, not what we might create together.

Response ability is different. Those who have it set their eyes on the future, grounding their vision in new possibilities. Response ability enables us to create the classroom culture we want rather than repairing the one we've taken for granted. Response able people don't focus on who spilled the milk. They recognize the opportunity to get better beverages on the table. Even when they've played a role in whatever problem needs correcting, response able people know that it's their actions and not their guilt or shame about the past that allows them to make amends by doing good works.

Image 4.1: Distinguishing Responsibility from Response Ability

What can we do tomorrow to create a culture of response ability in our classrooms?

When students change their behaviors, their beliefs and values follow. Explicit instruction helps. The ideas below are change-makers. Consider teaching them explicitly, modeling them consistently, and shining a bright light on those who do the same. Catch your students being response able. Make them role models. Share their stories.

- **HELP STUDENTS RECOGNIZE WHEN BLAME, INCLUDING SELF-BLAME, IS UNDERMINING PROGRESS.** Eliot D. Cohen, PhD, is the president of the Institute of Critical Thinking and a principal founder of philosophical counseling in the United States. His contributions to our understandings of shame and blame include these four irrational beliefs, which may prevent students from being response able. Define them clearly, illustrate how they work with stories and examples, and invite learners to check their own thinking when things go wrong.

  1. If something is wrong, someone other than me must be blamed for it.

  2. Whoever is blamed for doing wrong deserves less respect as a person.

  3. It's okay to ignore, alienate, name call, and even physically assault those who have been blamed for doing wrong because they are lesser people.

  4. If I accept responsibility for any part of the problem, then I also deserve to be diminished in the same way.

- **MODEL RESPONSE ABILITY.** Rather than being directive or providing advice in the midst of shame and blame, ask questions that build forward movement and momentum. Examples include:

- What are our options?
- What can we control?
- What are all of the possibilities that we haven't considered yet?
- How might we practice response ability rather than assuming or assigning responsibility?

- **STEP BACK, OBSERVE, AND STRATEGIZE (SOS).** One of the most common coping mechanisms for compassion fatigue involves silencing, shaming, and ignoring those who require the most compassion from us. When we find ourselves tempted to act in any of these ways, it's an indication that our boundaries may need tightening. Step back, observe the situation from a distance, explore your thoughts and feelings about the situation, and strategize, in order to set clearer boundaries.

Image 4.2: Sustaining your energy for compassionate living

This is how we sustain the energy to practice compassion. When we bear witness to another's pain, we often want to fix it. And fixers will invest great time, energy, and resources in serving those who are in pain. This is rarely productive, though. Boundaries are not indulgences. They serve those in need as well as caregivers by ensuring that everyone involved is practicing self-care and personal response ability. This is empowering. Rescuing others is not. You will find additional tools for setting and maintaining healthy boundaries as a compassionate person in the supplemental resources folder for this hack.

◦ A BLUEPRINT FOR FULL IMPLEMENTATION ◦

Step 1: Cultivate an understanding of privilege.

Many of us identify with groups that are both privileged (for example, wealthy, male, heterosexual, white) and oppressed (for example, poor, female, homosexual, black). Exploring privilege is challenging work, as it forces us to reevaluate our beliefs about ourselves, others, and the world we live in. It also puts us at risk of self-blame and shame as we begin to realize the unintended consequences of not knowing what we do not know.

The following strategies, tested by Diane J. Goodman, EdD, enable everyone within a learning community to examine privilege in an atmosphere that is free of shame and blame. This is critical to learning, growth, and ultimately, change.

- Challenge everyone to complete a social identity inventory, in order to recognize the complexity of their identities. You'll find one method in the supplemental resources folder for this hack.
- Affirm all identities.
- Invite people to consider how their different identities influence their perceptions of themselves, how others

perceive them, and their status in the world.

- Illuminate how our differences matter, and clarify how privilege favors some while oppressing others.
- Demonstrate how people do not have to choose or even want privilege in order to experience it. Explain that this may be why some struggle to notice and own their privilege: If they did not consciously choose it, it must not exist.
- Define privilege as a systemic rather than an individual phenomenon, and illustrate how.

Step 2: Encourage supporters, not saviors.

We encounter saviors in film all too often: the straight, privileged, white person who swoops in to beat back the bullies, befriend the gay kid, clothe the poor, and save the people of color, who are all desperate for help. Examples of this trope include *Glory, Mississippi Burning,* and *The Great Wall,* a fictional recounting of Asian "history" that places white, male actor Matt Damon in a lead role. In her article, "4 Ways Americans are Taught the 'White Savior Complex' (and what We Can Do About It)," author Amanda Machado reminds us that American schools teach a predominantly Eurocentric curriculum, and we've grown accustomed to rescuing other countries whenever they are in trouble as often as we start wars within them in the name of freeing people from oppression. As more and more people begin volunteering in other countries, many question their purposes and intentions. Rather than serving in ways that enable the served to help themselves, it's not uncommon for sentimental white people to position themselves as heroes in order to satisfy their own emotional and psychological needs.

How might we make a difference? We can begin by educating ourselves, first and foremost by putting a critical eye on inequities inside of our own system. We need to challenge curriculum that focuses on Western culture and celebrates privileged groups at the expense of all others. We also need to teach our children about the role that reciprocity plays when working for social good. Both parties should benefit equally from the exchange, and the effort made should always come from a place of true service. We must follow the lead of those who are helping themselves and requesting our support, rather than behave as heroes. Visit the supplemental resources folder for this hack to explore resources, tools, and activities that can bring this work to life inside of your classroom.

Step 3: Challenge common notions about what it means to be an ally.

Mia McKenzie, author of *Black Girl Dangerous: On Race, Queerness, Class, and Gender,* recommends that those who call themselves allies lean in and listen hard to those who are marginalized, rather than turning up their own volume. She compels them to seek abundant, diverse voices, too. McKenzie questions those who blanket their identities in being allies, reminding all of us that our choice to be in solidarity with anyone does not make us an ally. Earning the trust of those we stand in solidarity with is far more important, and trust is gained and lost moment by moment. Context matters, and it's also a shapeshifter. Missteps will be taken, and when they are, apologies and amends will need to be made. Helping students anticipate and prepare to navigate these scenarios is important work. How might we help them seek diverse perspectives, listen and learn from those who are different from them, and take consistent action, knowing that they may likely be criticized along the way?

Efforts to perform and seek recognition as allies also compromises trust. How might we truly gain it? Begin by helping students start conversations about privilege, racism, and other inequities with those who *share* their identities. Help them become change agents inside of their own system. Most importantly, do this work yourself. You'll find a bit of inspiration and ideas that can support these efforts in the supplemental resources folder for this hack.

◦ OVERCOMING PUSHBACK ◦

Our profession empowers us to serve those who are marginalized and to notice and address inequities in our system. We may be one of few within our schools to own this power, and when we fail to use it for good, we exacerbate the problem. Perhaps you're grappling with thoughts like these or you know someone else who might be. They're common to many who struggle with privilege, and shaming ourselves or others for possessing them is usually counterproductive. How might you challenge assumptions like these in ways that are compassionate and respectful? Here are a few thoughts.

Marginalized people often take offense when none was intended. While it may feel inappropriate to take responsibility for unintended harm, compassion calls us to embrace response ability, especially when we feel misunderstood and even defensive. So often, our intentions are not aligned with the impressions we make upon others, and when offense is taken, our explanations rarely compensate for much. Owning our ignorance, listening to the needs of those we've offended, and changing our behavior typically does, though.

There is no such thing as privilege. It's difficult to notice privilege when we don't choose or enjoy it, but upon closer inspection and reflection, most white people are able to recognize the advantages and perks that they are entitled to simply because they are not people of color. For instance, white people do not need to fear racial profiling while driving or what might happen when law enforcement pulls them over. In general, assumptions are not made about the socio-economic status, job performance, speaking skills, or fashion preferences of white people based upon the color of their skin. The writers at Teaching Tolerance remind us that when white children cut their fingers at school, the bandages they receive from the nurse will likely match the color of their skin, and when those same children vacation with their parents, the complimentary bottles of shampoo provided by their hotels will likely work with the texture of their hair. You will find additional examples of privilege and a variety of resources that will help examine your own and explore it with students in the supplemental resources folder for this hack.

Maybe if kids were more responsible, I wouldn't have to model response ability. Very few people are responsible all of the time, especially young people who are inexperienced in the world and whose brains are not yet fully developed. Most responsible students are supported by parents and other caring adults who consistently model this for them. Those who don't are relying on you to show them the way. This may be your opportunity to make a difference for those students who have not enjoyed the privileges that others have. It may also be an opportunity for you to demonstrate healthy and compassionate ways to respond to those who do not behave responsibly. While shame and blame might help you discharge the frustration that's inherent in experiences like these, the relief that follows is almost always temporary. What's worse, failing to model response ability will increase the likelihood of future irresponsibility and the likelihood that other children will begin to use shame and blame in their exchanges with one another.

○ THE HACK IN ACTION ○

Peter Anderson, a white seventh-grade English language arts teacher from Arlington, Virginia, made the same discovery about himself in the wake of the deadly alt-right rally that took place in his home state during the summer of 2017.

"Charlottesville kick-started my desire to fight for racial justice," he explained. "Watching young white men chant Nazi slogans in the open was too vile to ignore. It's worth noting how ridiculous this is. People of color, especially black American men and women, are murdered by the police on a weekly basis. There is no shortage of black death. Yet it took white men with torches broadcasted on continuous loop to shock me out of my white silence and racial complacency."

When the news cycle reset a week or two later, he admits that he noticed his attention drifting, though. "Because of my white privilege, I've never had to grapple with issues of race," he continued. "I've had to make a conscious decision to keep images of racial injustice in front of me at all times, in order to resist the narcotizing pull of white supremacy culture."

Peter knows that white people aren't often able to have informed discussions about race, class, and gender. "We've built an environment that insulates us from these conversations," he says. "For the most part, we live, work, and enter into relationships with other white people. We feel entitled to extreme racial comfort at all times."

Most importantly, he realizes that the white students he works with are experiencing the same socialization. "As a teacher, this silence is further exacerbated by my field's dominant ideologies. We're socialized to view curriculum, instruction, and our status as professionals as politically neutral. We come in, observe, diagnose, and prescribe with little consideration of what we're doing and why we're doing it beyond neutralizing rhetoric of 'what's best for all learners.' High-stakes testing, tracking, certain strains of personalized learning, and data-based surveillance are simply a few of the activities we participate in that can negatively impact students of color."

Peter realizes that cultivating authentic ally-ship, critical consciousness, and anti-racist dispositions must begin inside of classrooms, but that teachers must be the first to gain an education.

"The first step of raising my own critical consciousness has come in the form of self-guided research. There is no shortage of reading material; critical race scholars have been publishing books and articles about whiteness, white supremacy culture, and anti-racist pedagogy since the 1990s," he reminds us, and you'll find a link to recommended readings in the supplemental resources folder for this hack.

Another simple but profound practice? "Follow only people of color on social media," Peter suggests. "Listen to them, read the articles and threads they boost, and keep yourself out of conversations. It took multiple black women calling me out for entering into spaces I wasn't wanted or needed before I was able to begin internalizing the message that not everything is for me."

Peter also encourages us to begin providing payment for the intellectual and emotional work of people of color. "When you come across an article that you find helpful, spend sixty seconds looking for a way to remunerate the author," he suggests. "Support social justice groups such as Black Lives Matter and Showing Up for Racial Justice as well."

All of these activities help privileged people reorient themselves to inequity and, more importantly, behave in ways that perpetuate justice. Peter has discovered that this isn't enough, though. We need to figure out which work is ours to do and when our desire to help does more harm than good.

"The urge to rush in and claim ourselves as allies often comes with white supremacy baggage," he warns, "but teachers have the ability to create classrooms that decenter whiteness. We have the power to center the lives, voices, and experiences of people of color where they rightfully belong inside of our systems." If you're interested in considering the theoretical shifts that inspire Peter's own work in this arena, you'll find a useful table in the supplemental resources folder for this hack.

"Paradoxically, the more I center whiteness as an object of study in my own life, the easier it is to decenter it in the classroom," he tells us. He's invited other white teachers to join him in this study as well. "I started a social justice education group for other teachers in my school." Peter encourages others to do the same. "Gather a racial caucus of white teachers in your own school. Read things written by people of color. Strategize ways to compassionately call each other out and hold everyone accountable."

Peter acknowledges that this isn't quick or easy work. It's uncertain and uncomfortable. It's also the work of a lifetime. "We must subject our curriculum, our assessments, and school policies, and our own biases to rigorous critical analysis," he explains. "We must teach and model this critical inquiry with our students, too."

How might we help students discuss their own racial identity? Teach them about privilege? Ask them to interrogate the what, why, and how of their own schooling experiences?

How might we help them connect what they're learning with what's happening in their lives inside and outside of our classrooms?

"We need to do our own work first," Peter tells us. "We can't ask our students to commit to social justice work without doing this ourselves. We have to know our stuff."

We have to be willing to own it, too.

Bill Ferriter's experiences as a parent heightened his sense of response ability in his own classroom. "I know full well that my kids' strengths don't align with traditional definitions of success in school," he revealed on his blog, The Tempered Radical, in August 2017. "I'm dreading the inevitable phone calls from school employees, telling me my kid isn't working as hard as she can, isn't sitting in her seat as quietly as she can, or isn't making as many friends on the playground as she can."

When Angela spoke with him several months after this post went live, he admitted that his fears have become a reality.

This is what inspired him to make several promises to his own students and their families, the least of which included a commitment to consistent celebration. "I'm going to celebrate every child," he explained. "Whether it's writing letters directly to the parents or making Kudos cookies, I plan to praise all that is unique and amazing and important about your kid, even if they are struggling academically or socially in my room."

Bill tells us that kids deserve this and parents do too.

What's most interesting is the positive effect that this pledge to praise has had on him personally. "When I start the day deliberately naming the strengths of my students, their weaknesses don't leave me frustrated," he reflects. "I'm far more tolerant when the wheels fall off the bus during the course of the day."

This is what response ability in action looks like.

It's what a compassionate classroom looks like, too.

As we come to recognize and understand the root of our privilege and its influence in our small and larger worlds, our ability to shift from a place of responsibility to one of response ability improves. The supplemental resources folder for this hack includes additional readings, research, and activities that can help you navigate this work with the learners you serve. There, you will find:

- Additional resources for examining privilege with your students
- Peter Anderson's theoretical shifts and recommended reading list
- Additional perspectives from Eliot Cohen, PhD, Diane J. Goodman, EdD, Amanda Machado, and Mia McKenzie

Supplemental resources for Hack 4

EXTINGUISH SHAME

Reframing Vulnerability

*I've learned that people will forget what you said, people will
forget what you did, but people will never forget
how you made them feel.*
—MAYA ANGELOU, AMERICAN POET, MEMOIRIST AND CIVIL RIGHTS ACTIVIST

○ THE PROBLEM: WE ARE QUICK TO JUDGE OUR STUDENTS ○

Whether we like to admit it or not, teachers have the potential
to have a profound and lasting effect on our students.
Sometimes we are remembered in ways that belie our best
intentions. Ellen tells a story of when she was in AP American history
class, more than 40 years ago. The teacher liked to call out students
when they weren't performing up to his expectations of how they
should be participating in his class. For him, classroom discussion was
of great value, as he believed we learn best from a free interchange of
ideas and interpretations of the readings. She vividly remembers how
this teacher, in his desire to encourage participation, shamed a very
quiet and anxious student when he said, in front of the whole class,

"Robert, we haven't heard from you at all this semester. I think I'll replace you with a potted plant!" To this day, her heart palpitates and she feels the tightness in her abdomen as she recalls this embarrassing event. And the shaming wasn't even directed at her! It turns out that this student was painfully shy, extremely anxious, and the victim of teasing and bullying because he was so socially awkward.

When teachers shame students, or peers shame each other, trust is broken and connection is eroded.

Another experience Ellen recounts is that of one of her childhood friends, whose third-grade teacher made him stand in the garbage can on a regular basis, in the corner of the classroom, because he fidgeted in class, appeared uninterested in the lesson, and spent more time gazing out the window than completing his work. The teacher had decided that this student would never succeed and the only job he was fit for was as a sanitation worker, and she felt it was her responsibility to make a point of that to the whole class. Ellen and her friend now laugh about this incident more than 50 years later, but the emotional trauma this teacher caused remained fresh for a long time and greatly affected his self-confidence in his own academic abilities. (Fortunately, that didn't stop him from becoming the head of one of the world's leading foreign policy think tanks after attending an Ivy League college and earning a PhD.) What his third-grade teacher didn't realize at the time was how bored he was with the lessons she was teaching and how he needed greater intellectual challenges to keep him focused. She also failed to realize that he was a naturally deep thinker, who would always be more engaged by what was going on inside his head than what was happening around him. Nonetheless, she was quick to judge, and relied on shaming to try to whip him into shape.

These examples of shaming and humiliation are extreme and tantamount to child abuse. Most of us are well meaning and would never intentionally hurt a student by shaming them with our words or actions. But classrooms are by nature potentially shaming places where students are subject to judgment, evaluation, assessment, grading, scoring, comparison, criticism and scrutiny for how they perform, behave and stack up against the rest, and what they say, do, and reveal about themselves on a daily basis. That makes schools the ultimate in vulnerability communities and students continually at risk for shaming and humiliation.

Add to that the social environment where students are made to feel less than by their fellow students through teasing, bullying, and shaming. As the adults in the room, we must be sensitive to the many, often subtle ways that kids may treat each other badly, including saying and doing hurtful things in your classroom, as well as through social media. Many students are coming to class feeling ostracized, fearful, threatened, anxious, bruised and distracted by these emotions. It is important that we appreciate their experiences and acknowledge how those experiences may contribute to their reticence.

When we feel vulnerable and are subject to shame, we shut down, retreat into ourselves, feel unworthy, and become embarrassed and unproductive. When teachers shame students, or peers shame each other, trust is broken and connection is eroded. This can happen even when we are not conscious of the power of our words and are not being purposefully shaming. For example, it's common to hear teachers say things like "If you put as much time into your algebra homework as you spend playing in the band, you might be more successful." A comment like that is often meant to motivate a student to work harder, but in reality it makes them feel less than worthy, and inadequate. The teacher can reframe the comment with something like "I've seen you put a great deal of effort into practicing your guitar so you can play in the band. How might you spend more time studying for your math tests so you can master the problems?

How can I help you pass this course?" Often it's when we recognize and appreciate who our students really are that we can help them become the best they can be.

We need to reframe the way we think about ourselves and our students. If we acknowledge their vulnerability—and ours—we can operate from a place of empathy and compassion and open ourselves up to seeing our students as human beings who want what we all want—to be loved, accepted, and to feel worthy of succeeding.

◦ THE HACK: HONOR STUDENTS AS HUMAN BEINGS, NOT HUMAN DOINGS ◦

Dr. Brené Brown points out that vulnerability is a human emotion that is neither good nor bad. In fact, she sees vulnerability not as a weakness, but as the core of all of our feelings. When we shame others we are derailing their courage to be vulnerable.

The truth is that all students, no matter their age, grade level, academic ability, or apparent self-confidence, come to class feeling vulnerable. When we acknowledge them as human beings, with complex emotional lives like our own, we are equipped to help them prepare to open themselves up to real learning. Shaming not only disrespects them, but may also set them up for failure, lack of engagement, low motivation, and a perpetual self-defeating attitude. Learning entails taking risks, and it is our responsibility as teachers to create an environment where students can open themselves up to what's possible, to try to reach their potential and to be embraced for who they are.

When we reframe vulnerability as having the courage to take risks, to be uncertain, and to expose ourselves emotionally, that's when real growth, change and learning can take place. It is up to us to create an emotionally safe environment that is built on trust and respect, nurturing students' potential rather than shaming them.

There are a number of things you can do to shift the tone of your classroom to a more positive one. You have more power than you may think in creating a community that's based on safety and trust, where students feel comfortable enough to open themselves up to learning. Here are some suggestions:

- **PRACTICE VULNERABILITY.** Show your students you are vulnerable to being judged and shamed, just like they are. If you reveal yourself to them, they will open themselves up to letting you know them. On the first day of class, Larry Schwarz, whose story we shared in Hack 2, tells his students that who they see now is not who they will see tomorrow, in a week, in a month, or at the end of the semester. "Right now, who you see is an overweight, older man, and you may be thinking things and making certain assumptions about me that you will find out are not true as you learn more about me and spend more time in this class." When we admit we are all vulnerable, and reframe our vulnerability as an opportunity for authentic human connection, we have the potential to form healthy, positive teacher-student relationships of trust that foster learning on all levels—academic, social and emotional.

- **ILLUMINATE POTENTIAL SOURCES OF SHAME.** By shining a bright light on what students may be worried about when they come to class as well as what they most wish for, we can normalize their feelings of vulnerability and begin to treat them with respect. Angela uses an exercise called "Wishes and Worries" when she works with students to assess their interests, their needs, and their fears, and to understand that they are not alone in their feelings. She also uses what the students reveal to create agreements about how they will treat one another in class, and from time to time returns to the wishes and worries theme to check in on how she is keeping her promises to fulfill their wishes and create a space where their fears can be allayed. We have provided a protocol for Wishes and Worries for you to download, in the supplemental resources folder for Hack 5.

Image 5.1: Students reveal what they're worried about and what they wish for in class.

- **LEVERAGE STRENGTHS OVER WEAKNESSES.** When we take the long view of success, a student's academic accomplishments are less important than the character strengths they exhibit. Taking a strengths-based perspective helps us see our students for who they are, rather than for what they produce, create, or achieve. A strengths-based approach assumes that each of us are already good enough, since the goal is to cultivate our character and put our strengths into action. Remember that most students want to please you and will always feel "less than" if they feel they have to be perfect academically, or perfectly behaved.

- **CONNECT BEFORE YOU CORRECT.** Teacher-student relationships are built on trust and empathy. Get to know our students' interests and needs, while allowing them to know us. When there's connection, your students will trust you to offer correction. For many of us, our automatic reaction to our students making a mistake or misbehaving is to say or do something that shines a light on what they did wrong and criticize them. Instead, we can choose to remind them of past appropriate behavior and let them know you think they are ready to behave appropriately again in this situation.

  One of the best ways to connect with your students is to show them that you appreciate what they've done right in the past and give them a vote of confidence by showing them you believe in them—that they're capable of making good choices. The clearer you are in telling them what worked for them before, the greater the chance they will rise to the occasion. Make your compliment criteria specific. For example, "You really concentrated on building your robot and didn't get distracted while other students were having a loud discussion at the next table. How might you focus on completing your journal writing without getting distracted by the kids playing soccer in the field outside the classroom window?"

- **PROMPT POSITIVELY.** Choose positive words when communicating with your students about their potential. When you assess a student's progress with specific constructive feedback that's grounded in positive reality, you are offering them useful feed-forward that they can build upon. Even when you're attending to flaws, it's possible to frame your feedback in a way that builds your students' confidence. Rather than saying "This is where you need to improve," consider using "This is what you're showing me you're ready to try next."

Positive Prompting

Reframe your feedback to build energy with your students.

Instead Of....	*Try....*
You need help with....	You are showing me that you're ready to try....
You need to edit this....	When you're ready to tidy up your mechanics, I can help you. The content matters more though, and you're impressing me with.....
Please fix this.....	I notice you did x really well. Now, can you try y?
This is where your weaknesses lie.....	Where do you think I can best help you?

Image 5.2: Sentence Frames for Prompting Positively

Step 1: Perpetuate the notion that attitudes, behaviors, beliefs and values are fluid, not fixed.

There's been a lot of talk about growth vs. fixed mindset in education over the past several years. As teachers, whether and how much we show our students that we believe in their potential to learn and grow is critical to our students' view of themselves. If we shame them by telling or showing them that we believe they can't succeed academically or behave appropriately, we are perpetuating the notion that their abilities are fixed. A fixed mindset leads to decreased motivation and lack of willingness to put forth effort to improve. When we accept our students' vulnerabilities and acknowledge the fluidity of their attitudes, behaviors, beliefs and values, we are communicating to them that we believe in them and their capacity to change.

Step 2: Adopt positive discipline approaches.

Classroom culture is built on relationships. We are all hardwired to connect, and students, especially younger ones, come to class with need to please. Even the most seemingly reticent and most disruptive students want to be accepted and feel part of the community. Rather than tearing students down, we can lift them up and give them hope that they are capable of behaving appropriately and achieving academically.

Positive discipline is founded on developing mutual respect and believing in our students. It also starts with empathy, understanding our students' beliefs behind their behavior, appreciating where they are coming from, and working to change their beliefs about themselves in addition to their behavior. To discipline positively, we seek solutions rather than punishments. Positive discipline empowers our students to change their behavior and their views of themselves and us. And it builds trust.

Marva Collins was a teacher in South Side, Chicago in the 1970s. She later founded her own prep school on the belief that all students, even those most at risk from the poorest neighborhoods, could achieve if they were educated in an environment of positive discipline. Marva Collins' way was believing in her students and showing it. She set the bar high for each of her students, and one by one they met it, in their own time. Her approach to discipline was to remind them of their capabilities and show compassion in her words and actions.

One way to give students hope and help them believe in themselves is to teach them the power of "yet." We can point out to them that they may not be showing mastery of something or behaving up to standards "yet," and make sure they know that we believe that they can and will when they are ready. Encouraging our students, versus praising them, is motivating and nurturing without giving them false hopes. We shift them from self-shaming beliefs such as "I'm dumb" or "I'll never get this" to empowering attitudes like "The teacher believes I can do this if I keep trying," and "I'm worthy of succeeding."

Step 3: See and listen to your students and shape the environment around them—ask them what they need, and adjust the environment in response to what you discover.

Compassionate classrooms are spaces where people are allowed to risk being themselves and honored for the individual strengths and gifts they bring to their classmates. When we shut them down by exploiting their vulnerabilities or allowing others to, everyone loses the benefits of what they have to offer. The problem is that when kids reveal who they really are, they often challenge traditional notions of what school is, how students should behave, and how teachers should respond when they don't act in ways we expect them to.

When kids fail to respect the boundaries we set for our students, we tend to punish them. What if our boundaries disregard their needs, though?

When Angela was a new teacher, she was a stickler for the rules—especially the ones that planted students firmly and quietly in their seats, where they were to wait on her instruction. She embraced cooperative learning and differentiated instruction, but these experiences were carefully managed and led by her own assumptions about who her students were and what they needed rather than any interests or needs they expressed to her. It took many years and countless missed connections for her to realize what could be gained by allowing students to have much more say and greater control over how they learn, even if that learning didn't look the way she intended it to.

Now, as she leads writing workshops and facilitates makerspace sessions, she often finds herself in the company of kids who don't want to sit still or wait on her instruction. She's learned to honor their needs by paying little mind as they stand through her mini-lessons. She's also learned that not every lesson is necessary. Sometimes, she extends invitations rather than requiring attendance, and she encourages students to use the tools and strategies that work best for them as well. Over the years, she's learned much from students who use uncommon approaches. She regrets the opportunities she lost during the first years in the classroom. She gains a great deal of insight by asking students to tell her how her lessons were helpful on the way out the door and, more importantly, by asking them how she might make the next lesson even better for them.

Step 4: Acknowledge progress and avoid comparison.
Rather than comparing learners to one another, help them measure their progress toward specific learning targets. Make your descriptions of growth respectful, too. Rather than describing students as failures, define them as beginners. Rather than stating that they are below a standard, reframe your perspective and your words. They're approaching it.

Step 5: Consider the unintended consequences of ranking.

When teachers within and across diverse systems are able to translate and attend to standards in wildly different ways, grade point averages are inequitable. When the practices used to assess, measure, and average grades are different, grade point averages are inequitable. The same is true when teacher expectations regarding mastery and how children might achieve it vary. When we rank children by grade point average, we inevitably resort to sorting rather than seeing them. Standards-based grading can help us provide learners criteria-specific feedback and assess in healthy ways without resorting to ranking. If this is something that interests you, you'll learn more about it in the supplemental resources folder for this hack.

◦ OVERCOMING PUSHBACK ◦

We expect that many people who are familiar with what really goes on inside the classroom will call you a "Pollyanna" for trying to focus on the positive. But as the story goes, Pollyanna, with her positive attitude, changed the outlook of an entire town. Wouldn't you rather be a Pollyanna than a Scrooge?

I tried being positive, but it isn't making a difference. Behaviors, attitudes, and expectations take time to shift, and students need to trust the consistency. Consistently apply positive approaches for some time before students settle in and trust you and the process. It's about creating and sustaining a positive classroom culture. If you keep asking yourself what's working and iterate on that, you are moving in the right direction.

Our education system doesn't function this way. We need to prepare our students for a "cruel" world by "inoculating" them with comparison and criticism. Classrooms don't work like vaccinations, where you give children a small dose of a pathogen in order to protect them from getting the full-blown disease when they are exposed to it in the future. The tone we set in our classrooms allows students to feel good about themselves, be motivated to learn and achieve, and ultimately flourish. Cutting them down and shaming them is counterproductive to positivity in the short and long term.

Students need to know they are not the ones in control. If our goal is to change our students' behavior, making them feel badly is not the way to do it. It's more effective to build a relationship of trust with students and show them you believe in their ability to self-regulate and control their own behavior. When we see ourselves as facilitators of learning, and self-compassion guides who set the example for appropriate risk-taking, our students will behave in ways to please us and themselves.

Some behaviors are worthy of shame. It is never okay to shame, whether intentionally or unintentionally. When we feel shame, we feel even more worthless and our motivation to behave appropriately diminishes. We need to try to empathize with our students no matter how combative they are, or there will never be hope for improvement. One of our core principles is that all students are worthy of being treated with compassion.

Ranking is a part of life. That may be, but is it useful? Ranking is potentially shaming to those who are at the low end of the ranking. And, ironically, those at the top tier often feel guilty, self-conscious, and uncomfortable as well. Remember that we have the choice to create the classroom culture that we see as most compassionate. If we want a better world, we have to build it. This starts in school . . . we create the kids that will inherit the world. We help shape their values.

○ THE HACK IN ACTION ○

Ten years ago, Starr Sackstein began teaching English and journalism to eleventh and twelfth graders at the World Journalism Preparatory School. As a teacher in a traditional system, she became disturbed by the cutthroat competitiveness and lack of collaboration among her students. She observed how students were defining themselves and their worth exclusively through their grades, and not through what they were their learning. The A students flaunted their high-achieving status and held it over their less-than-A peers. Students who were getting grades of less than a 90 felt worthless, shamed, and less than, merely by virtue of the fact that they did not measure up. She wondered what it would be like for them if she substituted the grading system with a feedback system that featured constructive comments.

Starr was able to identify with her A students, as she was one herself. When she began to put herself in her students' shoes she realized that they were experiencing what she had as a student— there was nothing more important than achieving high grades. She remembered how her teachers constantly reminded students, "If you don't do your work, it's going to affect your grades." And she became ashamed at what she calls some of the same "abuses of power" she was "perpetrating against her students, unknowingly."

During report card season in 2011, Starr became acutely aware of the atmosphere of anxiety that pervaded everything at her school. What was notable to her was the anticipatory excitement that only the A students exhibited. "When report cards were handed out, there were either cheers or tears." When she came to terms with how she was about to grade her students with letters, she compared that to how her own son in elementary school was being evaluated through what she considered much more informative and reflective narrative feedback. She began to consider how she could better communicate her AP literature students' progress and learning accomplishments on their report cards. She wanted to change grading from an "isolated judgmental experience to a collaborative conversation." She felt that it was "time to give students the words to talk about their learning, in a meaningful way."

Starr brought more self-reflective student practices into class. And she began the conversation with her students: "What do grades mean to you?" At first there was frustration, especially among high performing students whose self-worth had been inextricably tied to their grades. She realized that "shifting the mindset around something like grades was hard work," but she refused to "slip back" into the strict letter grading system. As she observed the process, she saw her students "engaged in learning, pushing boundaries, and articulating growth in ways they didn't know teenagers could."

She attributes these results to taking risks and trusting each other.

The self-assessment no-grading system Starr has used with her students is continually evolving with the input of students. She continues to involve them in an iterative process of empathy, prototyping, testing, and refining as they go. It is collaborative and vulnerable, with everyone taking risks. And shaming is not an option.

Resisting the temptation to publicly ridicule and call attention to a student's misbehavior is sometimes difficult for teachers when they are trying to manage their class and keep them on task. When Ellen was observing Angela working with a group of elementary school students at a summer writing camp in Chappaqua, New York, she took note of how Angela handled a pair of twins who refused to engage and cooperate, and who were trying to trick her and the other teachers by wearing each other's name tags. Instead of scolding them for not following rules and mocking the teachers, Angela leaned in and tried to understand their need to take on each other's identities. She observed how they did everything they could to not differentiate themselves. When Angela paid closer attention, she began to notice that when they did allow themselves to stay on task, one of them was clearly more advanced than the other and felt uncomfortable showing up his twin. The more advanced one also had more impulse control than the other, but felt compelled to act up when his brother did.

Angela decided to confront the twins in a way that engendered trust and connection. She approached them at their work table, with other kids working around them, and said in a chiding tone with a big smile, "You guys have been working my last nerve, and you seem to be enjoying it." As they cracked cautious smiles, she offered a smile of her own in return. "I'm totally on to you." Pleased that they had accomplished their mission and yet poised for some sort of punishment or retribution, they were surprised when their expectations were not met. Instead, Angela proceeded to share a story of how her twin uncles used to fake out their teachers by attending each other's classes in high school, each pretending to be the other one. They ate the story up and all shared a good laugh.

From then on, the mood shifted, and the boys became more engaged—at first one more than the other. Angela had created the space for them to be vulnerable, one step at a time. It took the entire week for both of them to participate and own their own accomplishments, and there were some steps backwards as they made overall progress. But the fact that their behavior was not criticized or called out, and there was no shaming, allowed them to take risks to become known individually, and benefit from the learning opportunities that were offered at the writing camp.

For a deeper look at the issues of vulnerability and shame; social comparison and ranking; mentoring; as well as assessing and addressing students' Wishes and Worries, visit the supplemental resources folder for this hack, where you will find:

- Links to Dr. Brené Brown's books and videos on vulnerability
- Wishes and Worries Protocol (and videos of Angela using it)
- More about Starr Sackstein and her work on no grades
- Links to books and videos about Marva Collins
- A few articles about mentoring

Supplemental resources for Hack 5

DESIGN CURRICULUM THAT CULTIVATES COMPASSION

Beginning with Empathy

Cultural legacies are powerful forces. They have deep roots and long lives. They persist, generation after generation, virtually intact, even as the economic and social and demographic conditions that spawned them have vanished, and they play such a role in directing attitudes and behavior that we cannot make sense of our world without them.
—MALCOLM GLADWELL, JOURNALIST, AUTHOR, SPEAKER

◦ THE PROBLEM: PREFABRICATED CURRICULUM ◦

All too often, the quest to establish an aligned curriculum quickly and efficiently produces learning experiences that are stripped of personal meaning and relevance. Teachers are trained to understand alignment in terms of its relationship to learning standards that are defined by those outside of their system rather than pursuing required standards in ways that inspire shared vision and make students collaborators in the curriculum design process.

Angela enjoys supporting teachers through these processes, but she is always careful to remain program-agnostic. Experience has taught her that there are many good reasons to adopt curricula, but she also knows that most programs assume the interests and needs of learners. When teachers are encouraged to lift and drop prefabricated curricula onto their students, critical contexts are often disregarded, including their diverse cultural legacies.

According to Malcolm Gladwell, the author of *Outliers: The Story of Success*, a person's cultural legacy is defined by the attitudes, beliefs, behaviors, and methods for doing things that endure from one generation to the next. Our cultural legacies influence who we are, what and how we learn, and even the likelihood of our success in many arenas. Encouraging students to examine their history and consider its influence on their own values and beliefs is enlightening and empowering work that inspires critical thinking, a deeper awareness of bias, and the exploration of unintended consequences.

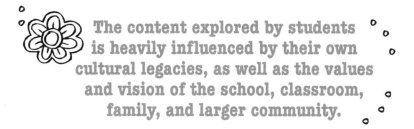

The content explored by students is heavily influenced by their own cultural legacies, as well as the values and vision of the school, classroom, family, and larger community.

When we design curriculum that cultivates compassion, we use dynamic frameworks that enable students to meet high standards and expectations while pursuing their own interests, attending to their own needs, and honoring their unique histories.

⚬ THE HACK: DESIGN AN EMERGENT CURRICULUM ⚬

Compassionate classrooms are fueled by opportunities to practice empathy, requiring us to treat content as phenomena that our students are experiencing rather than a collection of topics and concepts to be explored. Teachers provide opportunities for students to deepen their knowledge and sharpen their skills in order to be of real influence in the world.

Rather than merely consuming content, students who learn in compassionate classrooms produce it as well. This enables them to practice agency, develop mastery, and advocate for themselves and others. Students are seen inside of compassionate classrooms rather than simply sorted. Here, their histories make them strong, the challenges they face deepen their expertise, and their wounds become wisdom.

Emergent curriculum originates with children. It's responsive to their needs and interests, and guided by insights that teachers gain as they practice empathy. Units may have clearly defined outcomes, but the trajectory of learning is shaped moment by moment, as teachers observe learners in process, make careful observations, and talk with them about their discoveries, curiosities, challenges, and frustrations. The content explored by students is heavily influenced by their own cultural legacies, as well as the values and vision of the school, classroom, family, and larger community.

As teachers notice interests and needs emerging from learner's play and experimentation with content, they begin brainstorming approaches for deepening their inquiry and scaffolding the learning. Documentation and reflection are critical components of this work.

How might you begin using emergent curriculum in your own classroom? Define your long-term unit outcomes and learning targets first. An outcome is something students will know, do, or produce as a result of the learning that transpired during the unit. Meeting these substantial goals requires the integration of deep knowledge, various skills, significant time, and often multiple attempts and iterations. A learning target is a goal that students can meet within the space of a single lesson. Unit outcomes are achieved one learning target at a time. Targets are also framed in language that students understand

and find meaningful.

Once you know the outcomes and the targets you're controlling for, you'll feel comfortable allowing the rest of the learning to emerge from the experience. The recommendations below will jump-start your process and help you sustain and deepen this work over time.

◦ WHAT YOU CAN DO TOMORROW ◦

Design just one lesson. Image 6.1 illustrates the varied stances that design thinkers assume as they prototype, iterate, and improve upon a product.

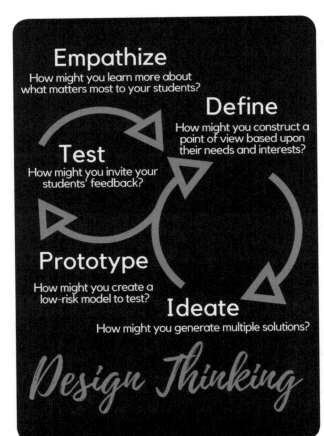

Image 6.1: Design Thinking is a Set of Stances that Inspire Creative Problem Solving

Recognize yourself as a design thinker and your curriculum as a product you co-create with your students.

Rather than lifting and dropping prefabricated programs into your classroom, know your unit outcome and your lesson targets, and sketch up a prototype: a low-risk model that is intended to be tested and learned from. Decide how you will practice empathy during the lesson and how you will use what is discovered to shape the learning and the work. Make space to pivot on your feet in response to the interests and needs that emerge. Anticipate how you might scaffold learners toward success, but don't act until you've verified that such scaffolding is necessary.

Document your journey, and reflect deeply. Once you've defined your unit outcomes and the learning targets for this first lesson, the ideas below will help you launch and learn from it. Be sure to visit the supplemental resources folder for this hack.

There, you will find protocols and tools that support each of the phases below.

- **EMPATHIZE.** In design thinking, empathy is a practice that enables those who are creating things to better understand and respond to the needs and interests of those they serve. It's not about taking on another's experiences or thoughts or feelings, but simply defining them well enough to be of service. Empathy drives emergent curriculum design, even within the space of a single lesson. How might you make your learning target transparent to your students and then access their interests and needs relevant to it?

  Once you've introduced your learning target for the day (for example, I can use scientific notation correctly), ask students to independently articulate their wishes for the lesson as well as their greatest worries. Then, invite them to brainstorm proactive measures that they or you might take to ensure that their wishes come true and that their worries aren't realized. They may do this alone or in small groups, depending on the culture of your classroom and how much time you have. Use what is shared to adjust your instructional plan.

- **INSPIRE.** Provide students abundant choice, diverse materials, and different pathways through the learning experience that are aligned to their interests and needs. Encourage them to pick the path that inspires them most.

- **ENGAGE.** As students sink into the learning, observe their processes, engage them in dialogue about the intentions behind the choices they are making, and interview them about their experiences and the resulting effects.

- **ITERATE.** Improve the learning experience in response to what emerges from it. Coach learners to change their purposes for learning, what they are investigating, how they are investigating it, or who they are working with. Help them refine or expand the questions driving their investigations.

- **INFLUENCE.** Document your most important discoveries by capturing audio, video, or photographic evidence. Gather student work samples. Make notes. Gather data throughout the process. Reflect on your own learning, and then prepare to share it with others who might benefit from it within and beyond your system. Many teachers enjoy using apps like Seesaw to support this work, but analog tools are useful, too. Michele Cammarata, a reading teacher in the Kenmore Town of Tonawanda School District just outside of Buffalo, New York, uses a sketchbook to document and reflect on her own learning. You'll find a page from her book in image 6.2.

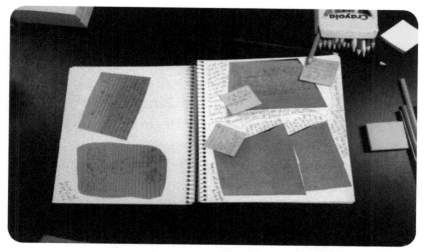

Image 6.2: Michele Cammarata uses a sketchbook to document
And reflect on her students' work and her own learning.

◦ A BLUEPRINT FOR FULL IMPLEMENTATION ◦

Step 1: Create a shared vision.

What if our greatest visions for teaching and learning were inspired by the children we serve rather than the experts who theorize about them? What if our students, the ones who are most directly affected by our vision, played a far more significant role in creating it? Vision is shared when community members, system leaders, teachers, support staff, and students play an equal role in shaping it. Vision isn't something that should be crafted in boardrooms and then sold to teachers and students. It isn't something we try to garner a commitment to, either.

Create a shared vision by inviting students and teachers to articulate their own first. Look for the trends that emerge from these individual statements—these shape the unique vision of each class. Place each class vision on a table or a wall, side by side with all of the others. Find the trends that emerge across those statements. These trends combine to shape a building vision. Place each building vision on a table or a wall, side by side with all of the others. Find the trends that emerge from those statements. These can inform your district vision.

It's powerful to include the right voices at the right time as visioning work unfolds. Teachers contribute to classroom vision, principals and assistant principals contribute to building-wide vision, along with support staff for each building. Assistant superintendents and superintendents contribute to the district-wide vision, along with board members and other leaders at that level of the system.

You'll find protocols and tools for facilitating shared visioning in the supplemental resources folder for this hack. Once you've defined what really matters inside of your system, you'll be ready to frame a year of learning inside of your classroom.

Step 2: Frame your year.
A curriculum framework is different from a map or a syllabus. It's a snapshot that provides an aerial view of the units that will be explored and the works that will be produced within an instructional year. You'll find examples of such frameworks in the supplemental resources folder for this hack. How might you create your own?

Step 3: Design aligned units.
A unit framework is a blueprint that includes the essential questions, outcomes, learning targets, and assessments aligned to one specific unit. It's tight enough to ensure that quality learning and work are

produced, but loose enough to allow plenty of student choice and varied pathways across the learning trajectory. You may visit the supplemental resources folder to explore examples of emergent curriculum unit frameworks as well.

Step 4: Iterate throughout the year.

As your experiences with emergent design evolve, your ability to pivot on your feet will improve as well. Recognize when you need to shift your approach in order to meet the needs of the students you serve. Invite them to do the same as they discover more about who they are and what they need as learners.

Step 5: Use your discoveries to be of influence in the world.

Sharing our expertise isn't about showing off. It's about giving back to the field and growing the good. Use what you learn from your students to be of service to other teachers and learners by making your work transparent, amplifying your discoveries, and engaging with others in social networks. Start a blog, share your updates on Facebook or Instagram, and participate in Twitter chats with others who share your interests and dilemmas.

○ OVERCOMING PUSHBACK ○

Teachers have traditionally maintained full control over the curriculum they teach. Making our plans transparent and inviting students to finesse them is uncomfortable for many. There are good reasons to question this approach. Here are the ones we encounter most often.

I'm required to follow a prescribed curriculum. If you're teaching a tightly-prescribed, mandated curriculum, this is all the more reason to begin identifying and attending to the emerging needs of the students you serve. How might you take care to assess student progress toward your learning targets in each session? Levels of engagement? Evidence of productive and unproductive struggle? This is all about paying attention and responding to what you notice. How might you document your findings in a way that leaders will find compelling?

If I embrace emergent curriculum, the quality of students' work will suffer. Emergent curriculum design does not put students at the helm of any ship, nor does it enable them to steer into muddy water. It's an opportunity for you to make the "must do" learning clear to students, assess relevant interests and needs, and invite them to take powerful off-road trips in order to improve the quality of their learning and work. If what's happening looks like anything less than this, it's important to re-evaluate your approach.

My students aren't self-motivated enough to direct their own learning this way. Constraints are key. Share your learning target, and ask them what they'd like to know more about or be able to do relevant to it. Teach your lesson, but invite learners to reflect before, during, and after learning, so that you may pivot as needed.

◦ THE HACK IN ACTION ◦

The physical education department in Wellsville Central School District epitomized the ideal of emergent curriculum practice when, upon realizing that many students were failing to participate in class, they practiced empathy rather than judgment. Over the course of two years' time, these teachers gathered multiple data points, including evidence gathered from observations of students who were at risk of not participating in physical education, and they used their discoveries to reshape their curriculum, providing different pathways to success.

It all began with the development of a meaningful departmental vision. For these teachers, achievement was not defined by singular examples of skill or strength. This group intended to design a curriculum that produced mindful, health-conscious, and empowered adults who could self-assess and set goals to sustain their well-being throughout their lives.

"Graduates of Wellsville Central School District will sustain a lifelong habit of assessing and attending to their personal health and wellness," their vision began. "They will graduate with skills and tools that enable them to assess their strengths and their needs. They will create goals that support lifelong health, seek the knowledge needed to accomplish these goals, and adopt new skills that support them."

Perhaps most importantly, "Wellsville graduates will emerge confident in their abilities to identify which choices serve their health, which ones do not, and which pathways they can take to advocate for themselves and seek support as they create and maintain vibrant, healthy lives."

Rather than attending to performance alone, Wellsville physical education teachers were eager to empower students to take control of their well-being in ways that were personally meaningful to them. Their vision was inclusive of all kinds of students, and it also invited student voice and choice.

Their vision prompted a close evaluation of their entire curriculum, the exploration of alternative approaches for earning physical education credit, and finally, the redesign of their evaluations. Rather than relying on testing and performance during play alone, teachers explored portfolio assessment. Students were invited to complete physical and mental well-being evaluations, to goal set, and to engage in inquiry work that would help them develop the knowledge and skills necessary to sustaining healthy habits beyond graduation.

Their plan put self-advocacy front and center, too. Teachers don't just expect students to identify and share their needs, they make learning how to do so part of the curriculum and a valued practice. This has a significant influence on school culture. If you're interested in learning more about this work and perusing the vision and grade-level outcomes created by this department, drop into the supplemental resources folder for this hack.

Claudia Fitzwater, an elementary Spanish teacher at Drew Charter School in Atlanta, Georgia, is working with her students to redesign their classroom over the course of an entire school year. She's identified and prioritized the learning targets that her students must attend to, but the framework is agile enough to flex in response to their learning and the needs that emerge along the way.

"Our project is called Classroom Redesign for Social and Emotional Learning, and it's grounded in design thinking," she explained. Students will identify the interests and needs of everyone in the room, prototype the space and the furniture inside of it, and use their discoveries to build it. "The main goal is to redesign the room from the students' perspective. We want to create a studio culture, and we want the space to be flexible and adaptable."

Students use eco-friendly materials and recyclables, or they repurpose or modify existing objects and incorporate nature to build the furniture and embellish certain spaces in the classroom.

"They've used a lot of cardboard from school purchases to build prototypes and even their final pieces of furniture," Claudia tells Angela.

Students partnered with Solid Design Solutions, a local company that makes furniture, to build one piece of furniture for the classroom.

"Our pieces will be built during a field trip visit to the company," Claudia says. "Ongoing conversations with the design team, owner, and students take place throughout the project."

Students assess the needs of the teachers and students who use the room. These users have also tested their prototypes. Google Docs and Forms helps them analyze their input and build surveys to gather better information.

"The redesign includes the construction of a peace corner that students have added as part of the Social Emotional Learning piece of the project," Claudia adds.

The work that's happening inside of this space provides students ample control over their learning and what they produce as well, even as they work toward shared targets. All of the students are designing digital narrative stories, based on subjects and events of their own choosing. They will also determine which mediums and tools might help them share their work with their intended audiences effectively.

"Each student will design his or her own unique storybook, journal, and puppet show. They will create their own content and make their own choices here. Some will use text while others use images, video, photography, or other media. Some might combine some or all of these," Claudia explains. "Literature, art, puppetry and technology devices will enrich language development and help students understand and apply narrative texts elements."

Final products will be shared with authentic audiences chosen by the writers. In Claudia's classroom, students learn Spanish in a meaningful way by using the language across different disciplines and settings, in order to produce things that are appreciated by others.

Claudia practices empathy so that her students might as well. You can learn more about her work and the work of other teachers who practice empathy and embrace emergent curriculum design in the supplemental resources folder for this hack.

Designing curriculum that is responsive to the emerging needs of learners may feel daunting at first, but those who have had the courage to embrace it tell us that it's soul growing work. When we take the time to truly know our students, they feel respected. They realize that they matter. They come to trust us and one another, too. You will find tools that will support your emergent curriculum design and implementation efforts in the supplemental resources folder for this hack. They include:

- Links to the best design thinkers on the web
- Emergent curriculum frameworks, design protocols, and templates
- A peek into Malcolm Gladwell's greater work
- An invitation to connect with Claudia Fitzwater and the Wellsville Central School District Physical Education Department

Supplemental resources for Hack 6

EMBRACE EXPERIENTIAL INSTRUCTION

Simulation, Role Play, and Authentic Learning Experiences

I hear and I forget. I see and I remember. I do and I understand.
—CONFUCIUS, CHINESE TEACHER AND PHILOSOPHER

◦ THE PROBLEM: PASSIVE LEARNING ◦

This is what Angela remembers about first grade: the single-file march into the building and up a silent staircase, where teachers waited for their students quietly in the halls, the quick left into the first classroom door, and the coat room behind her teacher's desk, where she was expected to hang her belongings quickly, without so much as a word, before reporting to her desk, where the day's work awaited her.

Morning messages were scrawled across the chalkboard, along with the names of the workbooks that sat in a tidy pile on her desk, and the pages she was to complete in each one before music or art class began. She learned to read a clock that year because the second hand was her only friend and the only thing that made noise in that room. She was grateful when her family moved later that year. She doesn't remember her teacher's name. She can't recall what she looked like, either.

This was the most glaring example of passive learning in her memory, but it wasn't the only one. Even her favorite teachers resorted to loading chalkboards full of notes that were to be dutifully recorded, memorized, and regurgitated on tests. It was performance, not learning, that mattered most then, and this is still the case in far too many schools.

Compassionate classrooms challenge the notion that knowledge is something that experts deliver rather than something that learners, including the teachers themselves, discover as they reflect on their experiences. This is critical for engagement, but there's something more: Experiential learning helps us manage compassion fatigue as well.

⊘ THE HACK: EXPERIENTIAL LEARNING ⊘

Sometimes, experiential learning is used synonymously with project based learning, cooperative learning, service learning, or situated learning, all of which are noble and worthy endeavors that can inspire active learning. Experiential learning is reflection-driven, though. It happens when we immerse learners in first-hand, concrete experiences and prompt a level of analysis that helps kids conceptualize what they're discovering.

Education theorist David Kolb's Experiential Learning Theory is founded on the premise that human beings learn by doing, as they move through these four stages:

- Active engagement in a new experience that provides opportunities for learning
- Reflecting on the experience

- Theorizing, in order to explain observations
- Experimenting with the theories, in order to problem solve or make decisions

A typical experiential learning event might look something like this: The learner chooses to actively participate in a meaningful and authentic experience, intentionally reflecting on what is learned throughout the process, establishing theories about what happened and why and how it will inform their choices moving forward. Then, the learner uses what is learned from these discoveries to enrich other experiences and experiment with them in diverse contexts.

How might experiential learning help us create compassionate classrooms? Take a peek at what you can do tomorrow and how you might leverage experiential education to build and sustain a culture of compassion inside of your entire system.

◦ WHAT YOU CAN DO TOMORROW ◦

Role play and simulation are two experiential learning approaches that most teachers can attempt with relative ease. The first involves assuming the role of a person or a character that we hope to understand better. The second involves recreating situations, environments, and processes, for the same reason.

- **CO-DESIGN MEANINGFUL, CONCRETE EXPERIENCES THAT PROVOKE EMPATHY.** Who or what do students need to understand better, in order to become more compassionate? How are they privileged? What kind of experiences might challenge and enlighten them? How might you create a simulation or role-playing activity that provokes empathy?

     You might begin by inviting learners to explore what they have and what they have not. Provide each student an index card. Then, ask questions that help them define the ways in which they are or are not privileged. Invite them to record what they have and have not on their index cards. Use the prompts in figure 7.1 to stimulate ideas if needed.

Exploring Privilege

- When you go to the store, do people believe you are trustworthy? Are you followed and watched carefully?
- If you are a boy, would you be ostracized for playing with dolls if you preferred to? If you are a girl, would you be ostracized for playing with trucks?
- Are you able to walk alone in the dark without feeling afraid?
- When you learn about American history, do you often hear stories about people who look like you?
- Do you attend school with people who look like you?
- Does your school staff include many people who look like you?
- Are you able to go up and down the stairs in public places easily?
- Are you able to visit any restaurant you wish, without fear of being unable to enter the establishment or get to your table?
- Are you encouraged to excel in every subject that you take?
- Are you comfortable using the bathroom you are required to use at school?
- When a question is asked about those who share your race, culture, or religious beliefs, are you the only one asked to respond to it?
- Have you ever been teased about your name?
- Do you have your own bedroom? Computer? Cell phone?

Adapted from the National Association of School Psychologists

Image 7.1: Prompting Thoughts about Privilege

Once students have compiled detailed lists, collect the cards and mix them up. Redistribute them, ensuring that everyone in the room receives a card that they did not create. This is the role that they will assume for the following simulation.

Ask students to assume the role of the character on the card they received. Explain that high quality monologues will not only reveal details about the person's privilege (or lack of it), but reflections on how their experiences with privilege might influence their perspectives as well as their behaviors. Invite students to examine their place inside of this simulated culture once all monologues have been delivered. Who appears to be privileged in ways that they are not? How might they feel about that? How could privilege be influencing class and school culture? What might we do to improve these dynamics?

- **ENGAGE EQUITABLY.** Allow students to remain anonymous by inviting them to type their lists or narratives rather than using their own handwriting, if they choose. Ensure that all learners have offered responses, and prepare a space for each of them on the line. Make sure that role assignment is random. Consider drawing cards, if you have the time. And let students know that this is a silent simulation. No one should speak, unless they're invited to.

- **COACH REFLECTION BEFORE, DURING, AND AFTER THE EXPERIENCE.** These frames are helpful:

  Reflect inwardly: How is the experience changing your thoughts, feelings, or perceptions?

  Reflect outwardly: How is the experience changing others' thoughts, feelings, or perceptions?

  Reflect back: How is the experience informing something that happened in your past?

Reflect forward: How might the experience inform your future choices?

When we share our reflections with others, they offer diverse perspectives and help us make connections that we might not otherwise.

- **TEACH THEM TO THEORIZE.** Once the role play or simulation is over, challenge students to use their reflections about the experience to create theories about problems they could be seeking and how they might solve them. Where might they practice more compassion? How?

- **INVITE EXPERIMENTATION.** Challenge students to act on their learning and to document their findings as they do. This would make for great reflective journal writing. Students could also build action research projects around the learning that emerges from role play or simulation, building a meaningful bridge between experiential and authentic learning.

A BLUEPRINT FOR FULL IMPLEMENTATION

Step 1: Seek systemic problems that experiential learning could provide solutions for.

It's not enough for today's learners to be problem solvers. If our intention is to shape compassionate citizens who are forces for positive change in this world, we must coach our students to become problem seekers as well. Where are problems hiding inside of your system? Which ones are glaring? Which should take priority? How might you use experiential learning to solve these problems?

Perhaps students aren't participating in physical education, and it's impacting graduation rate. Perhaps the school playground is in disrepair. Maybe your school has welcomed a large refugee population, and they are struggling to feel included. Maybe students are using social media irresponsibly. Perhaps there is unspoken tension between different social groups in your school.

Which problems require immediate attention? How might role play or simulation begin building a level of empathy necessary for problem solving?

Step 2: Activate students, staff, and leaders.

Experiential learning is as impactful in the boardroom as it is in the classroom. Students aren't the only ones who benefit from putting themselves in another's shoes. Sometimes, staff members and leaders are the ones who learn the most when systems commit to improving school culture.

Step 3: Engage in shared reflection and analysis.

Learning is social. When we share our reflections with others, they offer diverse perspectives and help us make connections that we might not otherwise. This is a critical component of experiential learning, especially because the meaning that we make is based on our own perceptions and informed by our narrow experiences. When we analyze them with others, we're able to access the voices of those who have personal, first-hand experiences with things we've only role-played or simulated. This helps us recognize and challenge our biases.

Step 4: Test potential solutions.

Action matters. If we engage in experiential learning and never take the opportunity to practice what we've learned, we'll never close the loop on the learning. It's when we act that we learn how accurate our perceptions and theories might be and how we need to change them. Testing implies experimentation as well. It's difficult to predict how a theory will serve others. It's important to gather evidence and use it to inform the conclusions we're drawing.

◦ OVERCOMING PUSHBACK ◦

Integrating experiential learning is challenging work. It's important to situate it within a broader context that supports your course, unit, and lesson outcomes. Otherwise, it will feel like an additional responsibility that you may not have the time or the resources to support. Experiential learning should bring your content to life, deepen students' self-awareness, and help them problem solve in ways that they find rewarding. Designing experiences that accomplish all of this requires time, patience, and experimentation. These are some of the biggest challenges that teachers face and our thoughts about overcoming them.

I have a ton of content to cover, and this has nothing to do with it. Experiential learning brings content to life. We study literature, music, art, and philosophy because all of them teach us how to be thoughtful, discerning, and influential humans who live with purpose and communicate with intention. Each memorable moment in history offers profound lessons in compassion. So does every work of literature, every song, and every work of art. Compassion is a lens that creates critical context for learners in every content area. For example: How might you use experiential learning to explore the role that compassion played in the decisions that historical figures made and, more importantly, the effects of those decisions? How might you use it as a lens that illuminates the power and purpose of math and science and the unintended consequences of practicing either without empathy? It's not enough to cover your content. Situate it within the study of compassion, so that it might matter. Make it stick.

Experiential learning can cause high emotion, and I'm not sure how to handle that. Protocols ensure equity, and they also create containers for the dissonance that emerges. Norming your conversations is important, too. Be honest with your students from the outset. Tell them that experiential learning might make them feel vulnerable at different points. Define dissonance, and share your own experiences with them. Then, engage them in collective boundary setting. Invite them to define all of the potential "hotspots" in the learning experience they are about to embark on. Challenge them to create norms that everyone will commit to following. If you'd like more guidance for this work, drop into the supplemental resources folder for this hack. You will find examples and lesson planning tools there.

My students won't take this seriously. They may not at first, and if this your experience, do your best to respect their discomfort. Anticipate a bit of silliness or even resistance, and meet it with compassion. Do not change your expectations, though. In our experience, students often welcome opportunities to role-play if the context for the work is one they're personally struggling with or have strong feelings about. They often want to play with it in a collaborative setting, and role play offers them a safe opportunity to do so. After all, they don't have to speak for themselves or reveal their own feelings or opinions on a matter when they've assumed the role of another. Experiential learning works best when kids have some skin in whatever game you're playing, along with opportunities to hide inside of someone else's. The learning has to matter, but so does the design of the experience. Structures that enable kids to uncover and wrestle with their own biases without experiencing shame work best. Others tend to disengage and even hurt them.

Ian Lewis is a third-grade teacher in John T. Waugh Elementary School in Lake Shore Central School District, located in western New York. Each year, he inspires his students to set collaborative norms by likening a classroom to a family.

"We can't choose who we share our classroom with," he explains. "It's our job to love each other the same way that we love our family." To emphasize this point, Ian led a math lesson that inspired students to calculate the amount of time they spent with their families compared to the amount of time they spent with their classmates.

"They realized that they spend much more time with their peers in class," he says. "This helped them realize how important it was to treat one another as family."

Ian coaches compassion with intention in his classroom. "We take some time to describe how different kinds of families handle conflicts, challenging issues, victories, and situations that come up inside of most households. Then, we discuss how what we learn from living in a family outside of school can help us become a great family inside of school."

This is how norm setting begins in Ian's class, and acronyms help. Students embraced SHIELD after searching for examples of each of its dimensions in their classrooms and schools. Ian took time at the beginning of the year to invite students to share evidence of how they and others in their system help one another stay Safe, behave in Helpful ways, become Intelligent, serve as Examples, act Loving, and remain Disciplined. He found that defining these words as his own expectations wasn't enough, though.

"Our morning meetings were important," Ian says. "Each day, we would explore a different characteristic and share examples of what it looked like in our school. We talked about more than doing our best to live like this. We also talked about how we could help others do the same."

Students in Chappaqua Central School District engaged in experiential learning in order to help those who were new to their community find rewarding ways to spend their time.

"When they researched our hometown on the web, they realized that most of the sites were written at very high reading levels, and the text was dense and disengaging," Ellen Moskowitz, instructional technology coach and professional learning facilitator, revealed.

The kids dove in quickly to create better alternatives. Dividing themselves into groups by interest, teams shot videos, captured images, surveyed residents, and even hosted contests and taste tests to determine which local hotspots were most preferred by the people who lived in their community. The web pages they designed were rich with visuals, written in an engaging way, and thick with hyperlinks that invited readers to learn more about Chappaqua from other reputable sources.

While Ellen was witnessing how experiential learning connects kids to their local communities, Dr. Jackie Gerstein was using it to help students of all ages become more globally minded. In her role as a gifted educator, she challenged fifth and sixth-grade students to research and amplify their own learning relevant to one of the 17 Global Goals found online at The World's Largest Lesson. As a part of this work, Dr. Gerstein used experiential learning to deepen her students' appreciation of wealth inequities.

As learners entered the room, the were randomly separated into three different groups—each tasked with building their own city. The wealthy were provided abundant, high-quality resources and food, as well the right to control the boundaries that governed their property lines and their behavior. The middle-income group was given a reasonable amount of good-quality resources and food and a comfortable amount of space. The lowest income group was provided limited supplies, a very tight space, and a small amount of food to share between them. The wealthy group was provided significant support as they worked to build their city. The middle-income group was provided reasonable support. The low-income group received little support and, in fact, found their rights and privileges infringed upon by those who were wealthier and more powerful than they were.

Image 7.2:
Wealthy builders construct their city.

The experiences that emerged from this lesson provoked thoughtful conversations about haves and have-nots, the distribution of wealth and power, the attitudes of the privileged as well as the poor, and the potential consequences of the redistribution of wealth and power.

When Angela spoke with Dr. Gerstein about the reflections that emerged during the debrief, she shared something revealing. "Each time I use this particular experiential learning activity with groups, those in the wealthiest group never share their resources or power with others." When this reality is pointed out to the students, their reactions have always been the same as well: The wealthy wonder aloud why those who are poor refuse to ask for their help, and the poor wonder why the wealthy refuse to offer it.

"This happens every time I facilitate this experiential learning activity," she marveled aloud. "It doesn't matter whether the class is comprised of adults or children. The wealthy don't think to share, and the poor don't invite them to."

This phenomenon inspires deeper thought and conversation as well.

To learn more about this activity, drop into the supplemental resources folder for this hack. You'll meet Dr. Jackie Gerstein there and gain access to her blog, User Generated Education. You'll also find her full lesson plan and supporting resources there.

Image 7.3:
Builders from the
low-income group
are confined to
inadequate space.

Compassion is difficult to decontextualize, and this is what makes experiential learning such a critical part of its success. Role playing and simulation offer learners easy pathways into this kind of learning, but when systems begin to identify the real problems they're hoping to solve, the learning that emerges from those experiences is profound. Consider how you might begin to help everyone involved in problem solving take a step back, reflect, and theorize. This provides powerful perspective. It also builds energy over rough road. When we remember that there is much to be learned from the experience, regardless of how challenging it may be, our priorities shift into place. We remember what matters. We focus on what might be gained from the experience rather than counting on the outcome. You'll find more ideas for supporting experiential learning and the research base that it emerges from in the supplemental resources folder for Hack 7. They include:

- A deeper dive into David Kolb's work
- Numerous experiential learning activities that build compassion in the classroom
- Reflection tools

Supplemental resources for Hack 7

HACK 8

TEACH THEM TO TALK BACK

Coaching Critical Questioning Skills

The important thing is not to stop questioning.
Curiosity has its own reason for existing.
—ALBERT EINSTEIN, THEORETICAL PHYSICIST, NOBEL PRIZE RECIPIENT

THE PROBLEM: WE VIEW BACK TALK AS DISRESPECT

Some teachers become overwhelmed when their students ask a lot of questions. They worry that diversions will interrupt their flow while they are trying to deliver critical content.

Other teachers become frustrated when their students don't ask enough questions. They worry that they are disengaged from the material, unwilling to debate, or generally tuned out of the learning process.

And many teachers are offended by disrespectful students who challenge their every move, question their decisions, and object to everything they are asked to do because they feel disagreeable.

When we practice empathy and ask ourselves what motivates a student to question authority, ask for clarification, challenge a point of view, or just send a signal that they need our compassionate attention, we may discover that what we most need to focus on as teachers is not the *why* but the *how* of asking questions and engaging in respectful discussion.

◦ THE HACK: HELP STUDENTS BECOME RESPECTFUL SKEPTICS ◦

We believe that daring to question is one of the hallmarks of a compassionate classroom. When a student feels safe enough to reveal themselves, they are showing they are ready to become engaged in the learning process. If we truly believe that it is our responsibility to produce curious students, we need to teach our students how to ask questions in ways that are appropriate, respectful, and productive. To foster their curiosity, we need to create a classroom environment that supports and encourages an honest exchange of ideas that lead to learning, work products, self-advocacy, and collaborative problem solving. We as teachers should be encouraging our students to ask questions, to become critical, and think at a deeper level than merely absorbing and regurgitating facts.

We as teachers have the opportunity—and responsibility— to help our students become more skilled at talking, thinking, and writing about issues from multiple perspectives.

Amy Edmondson is a Harvard Business School professor of leadership and management, whose research looks at how organizations learn. Much of her work is focused on how to create psychologically safe teams where members feel comfortable asking questions, offering ideas, and critiquing the status quo. She argues that in a classroom or workplace situation, whenever we have a question and don't ask it, we rob ourselves and others of small moments of learning. When we don't speak up, we squander an opportunity to innovate or contribute to creating a better organization.

So, how do we encourage students to become respectful skeptics? By creating an atmosphere of psychological safety. Edmondson suggests that it all comes down to three things:

1. Acknowledging that in facing uncertainty all voices matter and we are all dependent upon one another when learning to solve problems;

2. Admitting that we are all fallible and that we need to hear from every team member so we don't miss anything; and

3. Modeling curiosity.

Tech companies like Google consider psychological safety to be the number one trait of their successful teams. We are responsible for training our students to be the future workers and innovators in our society, whether or not they will end up working for a tech giant or another company that will require them to work in teams. For them to be successful, they need to know how to collaborate in finding solutions to tomorrow's problems. By arming them with the skills to be able to take interpersonal risks by speaking up and asking good questions, we are preparing them for their future.

We as teachers have the opportunity—and responsibility—to help our students become more skilled at talking, thinking, and writing about issues from multiple perspectives. And, as always, it begins with empathy and compassion.

Teaching students how to talk back in a respectful way and creating a safe space to ask questions and frame responses through verbal or written communication can begin with the following practices:

- **HELP STUDENTS REVEAL THEIR FEELINGS AND NEEDS.** Before students can speak up or ask questions or advocate for themselves, they need to understand what they feel, think and need. Our younger students may require a little more assistance than students in higher grades. Provide a structure such as sentence completion (e.g., "I believe in _____"; "I am struggling with _____"; "Right now I feel _____"; "In order to do well on the quiz I need _____"). By speaking in the first person, students will practice self-compassionate communication. You will find "The I's Have It" tool in the supplemental resources folder for Hack 8.

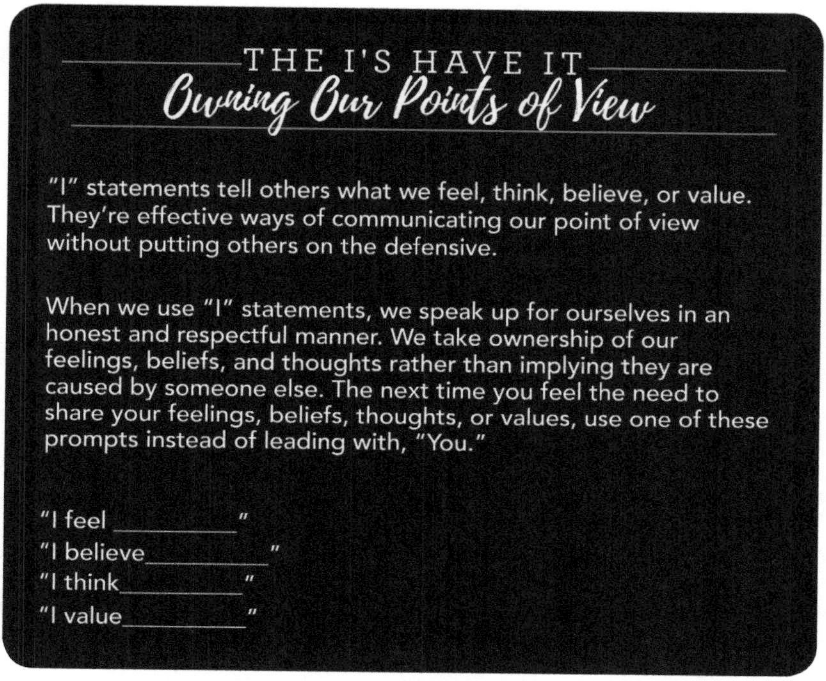

—THE I'S HAVE IT—
Owning Our Points of View

"I" statements tell others what we feel, think, believe, or value. They're effective ways of communicating our point of view without putting others on the defensive.

When we use "I" statements, we speak up for ourselves in an honest and respectful manner. We take ownership of our feelings, beliefs, and thoughts rather than implying they are caused by someone else. The next time you feel the need to share your feelings, beliefs, thoughts, or values, use one of these prompts instead of leading with, "You."

"I feel _____"
"I believe_____"
"I think_____"
"I value_____"

Image 8.1: The "I's Have It" protocol provides a structure to help students understand and articulate what they feel, think and need.

- **PRACTICE REFLECTIVE LISTENING.** When we practice reflective listening, we are using a communication strategy that is designed to make sure we understand what the speaker is saying by reflecting back to them what we understood them to have said. The first step is to listen carefully so that we fully understand them. The next step is to repeat back to them either a paraphrase or the actual words of what they said. "I heard you say . . ." In most cases, this makes the speaker feel understood. If we have misinterpreted them or reflected back to them incorrectly, reflective listening gives them an opportunity to clarify their point of view. Reflective listening can also be used to clarify a speaker's questions with "What I hear you asking is . . ." And it allows speakers to hear what they said from another's perspective, which may even prompt them to change their minds. Giving ourselves permission to be uncertain and to refine our thinking, or even end up taking the opposite position from what we expressed originally, is an important skill to develop.

- **FRAME YOUR RESPONSES COMPASSIONATELY.** As teachers, it is important to teach students to communicate clearly and compassionately by modeling respectful dialogue and using precise language. For example, we can teach students to clarify connections between ideas through phrases such as "as a result," and "however." By using phrases like "some people think . . . but I believe" or "on the other hand," we are teaching students how to respectfully disagree with others. Framing responses compassionately not only helps us clarify what we mean and avoids overgeneralizing and miscommunication, but it also helps us understand ourselves and others better. When we respond compassionately we are sensitive and open to the fact that not all questions require answers.

◦ **A BLUEPRINT FOR FULL IMPLEMENTATION** ◦

Step 1: Create a pushback forum for the adults and children in your community.

The intention is to invite people within and beyond your system to explore a challenging, even controversial issue together, with the intention to provoke, practice, and most importantly, get better at engaging in discourse. Which issues are causing the most tension in your system? How might resolving them improve school culture? Pushback forums enable people to share their stories, their concerns, and their diverse ideas within a tightly protocolled framework that ensures equity and safety.

Step 2: Establish boundaries and protocols to protect equity.

We designed the Lending an E.A.R. (Emotions, Appreciation, Reflective Listening) protocol for compassionate leaders who are ready to invite pushback on their ideas or decisions. Those who wish to push back may use the protocol to do so respectfully. You'll find other protocols for pushback forums in the supplemental resources folder for this hack.

LENDING AN E.A.R.

Encouraging Respectful Dissent

We designed the Lending an E.A.R. (emotions, appreciation, and reflective listening) approach for those who need to disagree but care about doing so respectfully.

Open a challenge by sharing your EMOTIONS about an issue calmly. For example, "I am worried that this policy may cause an unhealthy level of competition among our students."

ASK a compassionate question by APPRECIATING the leader's efforts first.: "I appreciate how difficult it was to reach this decision. I'm wondering if others could have contributed to the process in some way?"

Practice REFLECTIVE LISTENING by taking in the leader's response and offering it back, in order to ensure mutual understanding: "I'm hearing you say that you invited everyone in the building to participate in the policy design session, but only three people offered to attend. Is that right?

Image 8.2: We designed the Lending an E.A.R. protocol to encourage respectful pushback.

Step 3: Learn how to engage the right people at the right time.
Which groups of people would provide diverse perspectives and help you make better decisions? Who is most vocal and eager to be heard? More importantly, who has fallen silent in your system? How might you engage these people?

Step 4: Create opportunities for participants in the forums to set goals to improve over time and build community around doing so.
Make your greater purposes for the forum clear: Everyone in attendance must commit to improving the way they engage with one another around challenging issues. Which dispositions do you hope to cultivate? How will people know when they've been successful? Help them self-assess and set goals to improve how they engage over time. Do the same as a group as well.

⚬ OVERCOMING PUSHBACK ⚬

Inviting criticism and honoring the skeptics in any room is brave and important work. If you're hesitant, you're not alone. These are common worries. How might you overcome them?

It's my job to present information. Allowing students to ask questions that challenge the facts just wastes class time. It's our responsibility to help students understand what is a fact, what is an interpretation of fact, and what it an opinion or belief. In our current political climate where there are assertions from leaders about "fake news" and "alternative facts," it is especially important that students are taught to discern the difference between something that actually happened, and is observable and true, from something that "some people say" happened or "they heard." No matter what subject you are teaching, distinguishing reality from fantasy, fact from fiction, data from popular opinion, is crucial. Students must be encouraged to question at all levels.

I don't have time to entertain these kinds of conversations. These are the very conversations that constitute real learning and will prepare our students for success. There is nothing more valuable in any classroom than teaching students to talk back by modeling the skills they need to become respectful skeptics. Critical thinking comes about through inquiry and questioning. And the ability to think critically is one of the most important qualities that employers are looking for when they, one day in the near future, will hire our students. And critique of all forms is the primary business of the college experience.

Design thinking is based on asking appreciative questions, from inquiring about the needs of the user (students), to analyzing what worked or didn't work in the prototype we developed and tested, to knowing how to iterate. Questions are the backbone of learning and productivity.

I'm alone in this work. My colleagues are the non-example and model bad behavior. Yes it's sometimes lonely to be a maverick in your work and to be ahead of your time. But you know in your heart that by teaching your students to ask good questions in a respectful manner, they will be prepared to function best in our world. And at the same time you are teaching them to be compassionate listeners. Stay true to your values and set the tone in your classroom. For now, that is the only domain that you have control over. Your own behavior, and your own classroom. In time, your colleagues may even notice that the tone of your classroom and the demeanor of your students are worth looking at more closely.

We aren't ready to lead a pushback forum around a controversial issue. If you know that those within your system do not yet have the skills necessary to even begin these kinds of conversations, start small. Invite teachers to begin leading pushback forums and coaching respectful debate and civil discourse in the classroom.

Invite small groups of staff and community members together to begin this work as well. Add opportunities and extend more invites as norms are established and people grow into this work.

◦ THE HACK IN ACTION ◦

Ellen's late father, Seymour Feig, was a law professor who taught entertainment and intellectual property law at New York Law School. He was a huge fan of the Socratic method and ran his classes posing questions, telling stories from his own experiences with negotiating deals and drafting contracts, and encouraging his students to offer their own ideas. He had a practice of beginning the first class of every semester by writing the word "THIMK" on the board and nothing else. His motive was to spark discussion and get his students to question: Did he spell the word "think" wrong? What was the reason for writing this word? What did this have to do with the content of this course? That simple exercise set the tone for the rest of the semester. He never delivered content, but instead invited his students to ask questions. Although he had an outline of topics he covered, each class was guided by what the students wanted to discuss and what they needed to know in order to prepare themselves for practicing entertainment law. He built his entire class around empathy, listening to what his students needed to learn to become successful in their chosen careers, and structuring the curriculum and culture of the class around it. And he was the most beloved and highly rated professor at New York Law School at that time.

Influenced by her father's love of learning through open discussion, Ellen recently moderated a series of forums featuring LGBTQ high school students. Initiated by students in the Palmetto Alliance Club, and organized by their faculty advisor, Larry Schwarz, the first forum featured a panel of teens who identified themselves as falling somewhere on the spectrum of sexual orientation and gender identity; audience members for this forum consisted of students in the school community. The second forum included a panel of parents of LGBTQ students, open to any parent in the school community. The club members decided that the third event would consist of a more traditional presentation of information to teachers, with facts about such issues as social and emotional factors related to gender identity, coming out, suicide rates, and local and national laws affecting gender rights.

In an effort to engender an atmosphere of empathy and compassion, the Alliance Club members had decided that they wanted to create a space where other students, parents, and teachers could appreciate what it was like for them to be openly gay, lesbian, bisexual, transgender, and/or queer. For the student forum, the students came up with a series of questions that Ellen as the moderator asked them, and which they answered honestly. Questions included, among others, "How is your life different as an open LGBTQ person?"; "When did you come out to family? How did that go?"; "Have you experienced discrimination? Bullying?"; "What would you like the straight community to know?"; "How are people's expectations of you wrong?" Students in the audience were invited to ask their own questions as long as they were respectful. The interchange went smoothly and the panelists said that they felt heard and appreciated.

For the parent forum, LGBTQ students as well as parents of other LGBTQ students sat on the panel and the audience members consisted of parents from the school community. Again, using questions that the students had developed with their faculty advisor, and which Ellen used to guide the discussion, parents and students responded to such questions as, "What is it like to be a parent with a gay/lesbian/transgender child?"; "When did you share your child's identity to family? What was your experience coming out to friends?"; "How is your life different as an open LGBTQ parent?"; "What would you like the general parent community to know?"; "How are people's expectations of you and your child wrong?"

Although the students in the club are in need of having teachers as allies, they decided, at the suggestion of their faculty advisor, to provide them with an information session instead of opening themselves up to the vulnerability of a panel discussion. The teachers heard from a lawyer about legal issues pertaining to the rights of LGBTQ students, including gender-neutral bathroom policies. A school counselor talked about the psychological and social factors specific to being openly gay/lesbian/transgender, issues related to coming out, and increased risks for depression, anxiety, and suicide. Ellen presented the VIA strengths to encourage teachers to treat LGBTQ students as they would anyone else, recognizing and spotting the character strengths that we all share.

The feedback from that session was very positive, and several teachers told Larry that they were enlightened by the information that was presented, and sensitized to many of the issues that LGBTQ students face every day, which they were previously unaware of. It also resulted in adding more teachers to the "ally" list.

In the future, the Alliance Club would like to iterate on these forums, keeping the same format and adding questions based on what they learned from the inaugural run. In addition to an information session for teachers, they are considering having an open forum where teachers are able to ask students questions directly about their lives as LGBTQ students.

To learn more about teaching your students to become respectful skeptics, and for protocols to help frame good questions and engage with pushback around controversial issues, we have put a variety of useful materials in the supplemental resources folder:

- Team Building and Communication research by Amy Edmondson
- The I's Have It Protocol
- Lending an E.A.R. Protocol
- Pushback Protocol

Supplemental resources for Hack 8

HACK 9

INSPIRE ACTIVISM

Teaching for Social Justice

Action is the antidote to despair.
—JOAN BAEZ, AMERICAN SONGWRITER AND ACTIVIST

◦ THE PROBLEM: KIDS WHO CARRY
THE WEIGHT OF THE WORLD ◦

Compassion fatigue plagues children as often as it does adults, only many of them are less self-aware and unable to moderate the effects. Kids are sensitive creatures with unlimited capacity for empathy. Many are smart and savvy, too. They understand the magnitude of need that surrounds them. They witness it daily. It makes them anxious.

In fact, according to abundant research studies, today's kids are far more anxious than children were in previous generations. Why the change?

According to Dr. Jean M. Twenge of Case Western Reserve University, low social connectedness may be a factor. Americans are a proudly independent people, and as our understandings about marriage and work and family have evolved, we've grown more willing to be alone. This increased autonomy has created many healthier social constructs, but it has its drawbacks, too. We're more isolated than ever, and this makes us increasingly distrustful.

In order to feel at home in the world and in one's own skin, young people need to feel in control of their lives.

As educators and parents flock to psychologists offices, explore the benefits and potential side effects of medical intervention, and seek to understand how to best support this new generation of worried young people, some are considering an uncommon but powerful approach: social activism.

THE HACK: ACTIVATE, DON'T ENERVATE

Social activism is one of the only ways that people at the grassroots level of any system seek agency. In order to feel at home in the world and in one's own skin, young people need to feel in control of their lives. They need to have confidence in their abilities to moderate their thoughts and feelings, and they need to believe that they can make their world safe and their experiences in it satisfying.

We're inspired by young people like De'Juan Correia, who at the age of sixteen spoke against the death penalty to members of the British Parliament and at the Amnesty International Youth Summit. His motivations were incredibly personal, as his uncle Troy Davis was a death row inmate who was put to death by lethal injection for a crime that many feel he did not commit.

Social activism is a tall order for today's generation, and it's important for the adults in their lives to recognize this and openly acknowledge it.

Like De'Juan Correia, young people can increase their sense of agency by taking steps to change the things that trouble them most about their world. Helping them recognize how their individual choices influence even the greatest global issues is empowering for many. Creating opportunities for them to take deliberate action and notice the effects of their efforts can be healing as well.

○ WHAT YOU CAN DO TOMORROW ○

One of the most important lessons that we can teach young people is that doing good helps us feel good, but we have to balance our efforts carefully, in order to avoid overload. Here's how you can bring this lesson to life inside of your classroom and school.

- **DEFINE THE SOCIAL JUSTICE ISSUES THAT MATTER MOST TO YOUR STUDENTS.** This often takes some time. Invite students to read local, national, and international news. Make time for connection and reflection, too. Which issues are touching their own lives or the lives they care about most? Which ones are having the greatest impact? Who do they want to stand with? Why?

  As a black teen with muscular dystrophy, Darius Weems traveled across the country in order to raise national awareness of disability rights and the need for better wheelchair accessibility across the nation. His trip was documented in *Darius Goes West*, which elevated his voice and his message.

- **SUPPORT THEM AS THEY SEEK UNDERSTANDING.** This involves research, and few young people know how to do it well yet. As you guide their deeper dives into the issues at hand, teach them how to conduct quality online searches, and then introduce them to ethnographic research skills as well. Much can be learned from online sources, but inviting kids to immerse themselves in new worlds, make first-hand observations, and conduct quality interviews is crucial. Social action requires engagement. Connection diminishes despair. Drop into the supplemental resources folder for this hack to learn more about supporting this kind of learning.

- **TEACH THEM TO EVALUATE THEIR SOURCES.** Angela uses the four-step process outlined in figure 9.1 to coach source evaluation in classrooms. This is the work of many years, not a single lesson, unit, or grade level. How might you begin tomorrow? How could you invite others to help you scale the work?

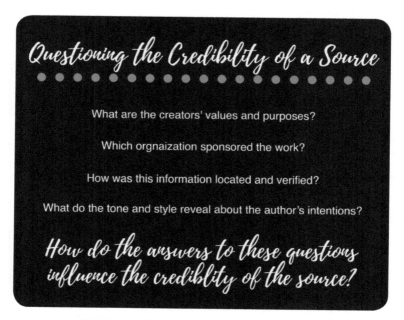

Questioning the Credibility of a Source

What are the creators' values and purposes?

Which orgnaization sponsored the work?

How was this information located and verified?

What do the tone and style reveal about the author's intentions?

How do the answers to these questions influence the crediblity of the source?

Image 9.1: Four-step Process to Coach Students to Evaluate Sources

- **COACH ARGUMENT WRITING AS AN OPPORTUNITY FOR PERSONAL GROWTH.** Sometimes, our research into an issue helps us discover the flaws in our thinking, and we realize we need to change our minds. We need to start over. This is something to celebrate and model for our students. Share your own stories, help students know how rewarding it is to change and grow, and elevate those who do as a result of their learning and social justice work.

- **EMPOWER THEM TO ACT JUDICIOUSLY.** Focus matters. Encourage students to work deeply for a cause that truly matters, and demonstrate the power of doing so. Many will be tempted to jump on every injustice. This is a struggle that most empaths know all too well; it's one that increases anxiety and depression rates as well. Tackle these realities head on, and help students align their work for social good to the greater vision of the difference they hope to make in the world. Help them see that when they do good work for their own reasons, it inspires others to do the same, and the needs they attend to may be very different. We grow the good through our example as well as our actions.

◦ A BLUEPRINT FOR FULL IMPLEMENTATION ◦

Step 1: Unify your school.

Earlier, we challenged you to design a curriculum that solves the problems your students face. In this hack, we're inviting you to let them do the same. Together. You might find inspiration in Zim Ugochukwu's story, too. This bold black activist founded *Ignite Greensboro* in order to engage her classmates at the University of North Carolina--Greensboro in honoring those who participated in the Greensboro sit-ins that were an instrumental part of the civil rights movement. How might you unify your school to act for a particular kind of social justice? What will your vision be? How will you achieve it? How might you create and, most importantly, sustain momentum for this work? You will find guidance and great inspiration in the supplemental resources folder for this hack.

Step 2: Align your year around a powerful act of social justice.
Timelines are motivating. They help us plan our work, assess our progress, and celebrate small victories along the way. How might you frame your year around an issue that matters?

Step 3: Impact change on several levels and several fronts.
This is crucial. When students can see change happening in their homes, their classrooms, their schools, their local communities, in their state, in their country, and on a global level, hope is born. Even when we fail in our efforts to inspire change, the attempt matters. Our commitment matters. The fact that we stand with those who need us and for things that matter lifts our students up. It gives them something to believe in. Addressing different forms of inequity through a single demonstration of activism is powerful as well. This is what Bryant Terry, a young black eco-chef and food activist from Tennessee did. He founded b-healthy! and challenged other young people to commit to creating a more sustainable food system. using "cooking as a tool to illuminate the intersections of poverty, structural racism, and food insecurity," according to his website.

Step 4: Assess your influence.
How will you know if your efforts are successful? How will you define this? How will you measure it? Be specific about what it really means to make a difference from the outset, and track your progress. The little victories along the way are often just as rewarding as meeting your final outcome. Sometimes, even more so.

Kids can't handle controversy. This is so true. In fact, many adults can't handle controversy, which is why it's important to do this work in schools. Kids have few opportunities to explore what controversy is and develop concrete approaches for engaging with it well. This work is one of our greatest responsibilities as educators. If approaching it makes you uncomfortable, reach out to us and to other teachers in the trenches on Twitter. Use the #compassionateclassrooms hashtag.

Kids shouldn't have to save the world. We agree. This is why it's important to help them choose which causes are most important to them and take action. This will ease their anxieties and their burdens. As Mother Teresa so famously said, "We can do no great things, only small things with great love." And this is enough. It has to be.

We can't impose our value system on our kids. It's important that we don't. Instead, let's create opportunities for kids to explore and refine their own, using quality questioning and productive protocols. This is how we inspire thinking without teaching students what to think. You'll find helpful tools in the supplemental resources folder for this hack.

⚬ THE HACK IN ACTION ⚬

When Angela's daughter Laura was 10 years old, she lost her grandfather and her grandmother within the space of a month, on the heels of a very turbulent year of family caregiving. She learned a great deal about cancer as her vibrant grandfather declined rapidly and died within months. A handful of weeks later, her grandmother invited her to visit. She told her silly jokes over lunch and talked about happy things. It was a very bright spot of joy in an otherwise devastating year, and Laura returned home beaming. The youngest of sixteen

Image 9.2: Margie Dintino's fifth-grade class from North Collins Elementary School in New York State begins a twenty-five-day kindness challenge with help from Laura Stockman.

grandchildren, it was rare for her to have her grandmother all to herself. That day was a gift in many ways. When her grandmother passed away unexpectedly twenty four hours later, her once predictable world seemed like a very uncertain and threatening place.

So, she started blogging. Christmas was coming, and Laura knew that she would be missing her grandfather, the sound of his harmonica, and the way that they would rough-house and play with her cousins. She wanted to bring him back for just a little while, so she made a plan. Laura decided to do a good deed each day from December 1 through Christmas day, as a means of following in her grandfather's footsteps, because he was known for his good deeds. She thought that perhaps honoring him this way would help her feel better. She wondered if she could inspire others as well by challenging her readers to do the same thing and offering a donation. She would donate that month's allowance to the reader who made the most difference for others in December. Her blog, Twenty-Five Days to Make a Difference, was Laura's way of making her world right again, even without her grandparents in it.

Angela was skeptical. She was uncomfortable with the social nature of the web, how transparent her daughter was being about her work in her space, and the number of people reading it. The effect was overwhelming, though. Thousands of readers participated in

Laura's contest, and many others offered to match her funds. Laura learned how many other do-gooders there were in the world, and the best of them reached out to help her find a bit of important balance, too.

When her first twenty-five-day challenge came to an end, Laura continued blogging. She started working for social good by volunteering with a number of kid-friendly organizations as well. That year, she learned a great deal about the kind of service work that energized her and the kind that drained her as well. This helped her make an important decision: She stepped away from her blog in order to visit classrooms, where she helped other children start their own. Laura continued this work through middle and high school, where she fell in love with design. Today, Laura studies design thinking at the Rochester Institute of Technology. She's carried the lessons from her social good experiment with her, including everything she learned about empathy, compassion fatigue, and the importance of doing small things with great intention rather than carrying the weight of the world on her shoulders.

Natalie Hampton is a high school student in Los Angeles, California. When she was in middle school, she never felt like she fit in. She was repeatedly bullied and physically attacked by other girls. She received death threats, was ostracized and cyberbullied, and sat alone at lunch every day. It got to the point where she was afraid to go to school, had trouble sleeping and eating, and even smiling became a daily struggle for her. Natalie didn't feel safe at school. She didn't receive any help or support from other students, teachers or school administrators, even when they witnessed other students visibly threaten and abuse her.

After applying and ultimately transferring to another school, Natalie encountered an entirely different school culture. In her TEDxTeen Talk, she recounts how at her new school "a boy stopped me in my school hallway and asked me if I needed help finding one of my classes—and it saved my life."

From that "simple act of kindness" Natalie fell into a group of friends with whom she socialized and ate lunch. But then a sense of guilt and responsibility overcame her. Feeling immensely grateful, yet at the same time acutely sensitive to her experience as a victim of bullying at her old school, Natalie knew that she had to do something to help other kids who had nowhere to sit at lunch, or were feeling voiceless and ostracized like she had. So she began inviting kids who were sitting alone to sit at her table. Natalie soon found out that one of the girls she invited to join her had been contemplating suicide, but that one small action of welcoming her to the lunch table completely turned her around from loneliness and despair to becoming Natalie's best friend.

Recognizing how the kind actions of one person can save someone else from "so much suffering," Natalie decided to create the "Sit with Us" app, a free mobile application that "takes kids looking for tables with friends at their school and pairs them together." Sit with Us enables students to have a safe place to have lunch, "without any fear of rejection."

Since she created Sit with Us, Natalie's good work has spread to hundreds of thousands of students, across multiple countries. She remains dedicated to inviting other young people to be kind to one another, and reminds them through her simple yet powerful message to students:

> "All it takes is one person to change the world . . . It's up to you to make a difference in your communities . . . Something as seemingly small as lunch can make a school way more inclusive, and something like a simple act of kindness can save a life."

Image 9.3: Natalie Hampton, creator of the "Sit with Us" app, encourages students to be kind to one another by inviting kids with no place to eat to join them at their lunch table.

When interviewing Natalie, Ellen asked what Natalie thought made her old school so different from her new school. Was it the students? Their backgrounds? Their socioeconomic status? How they were being raised at home? Why was she so mercilessly bullied at one school, and felt welcomed at safe at the other?

Natalie listed several reasons, which look very much like the definition of school culture. "The teachers and the administration set the tone," she said. "At my old school, they didn't have my back, and at my new school they do."

Both her old school and new school are private, comprising kids from homes with the financial means to pay the tuition. Each school has counseling resources to assist students with psychological issues they may be facing. However, at her old school, "the counselor blamed me for being bullied, and that made it worse."

She explained that at her new school, when students act out or in a mean way, the administration responds immediately and addresses it, as opposed to "sweeping it under the rug, and creating a culture of toxicity" like at her old school. In her old school "everyone felt like they could get away with anything because the people in power were allowing them to."

Her new school has a clear code of conduct, which they present to students at the beginning of the year, and remind them about throughout the semester. They discuss empathy and kindness in the classroom. They talk about "a lot of hard concepts like mental health," and that "helps the students open up."

"They deal with any problems as soon as they come up," and they point out what could have been done differently, so "they learn from them."

"When teachers notice what's going on and treat their students with respect, it kind of sets an example for all the kids in the class . . . and makes the students treat each other with respect as well."

Natalie thinks that the way teachers and administrators treat each other makes a difference too, as that also sets the tone. What the students see "trickles down."

"Even in high school kids are still impressionable," Natalie reminds us. "We still look to the adults around us."

Natalie's message to students can easily be applied to teachers too.

"All it takes is one person to change the world . . . It's up to you to make a difference."

If you're eager to explore the world of social activism with your students, you will find a variety of tools to support your beginnings in the supplemental resources folder. These include:

- A link to Laura's blog, Twenty-Five Days to Make a Difference, and its partner site, intended to help young bloggers begin their own projects
- A link to Natalie Hampton's "Sit with Us," social media pages, and her "All it Takes is One" TEDxTeen Talk
- Resources that will help you and your students learn more about social activism
- Tools for tackling controversial issues in the classroom
- Downloads that will help writers locate quality resources and evaluate the credibility of their sources

Supplemental resources for Hack 9

HACK 10

RESOLVE CONFLICTS

Restoring Compassion with Protocols

People fail to get along because they fear each other;
they fear each other because they don't know each other;
they don't know each other because they have not
communicated with each other.
—MARTIN LUTHER KING, JR, MINISTER, ACTIVIST, CIVIL RIGHTS LEADER

○ THE PROBLEM: WE TEND TO AVOID CONFLICT
AND PUNISH CONFRONTATION ○

As teachers, we feel responsible, and sometimes even pressured, to look out for conflicts among students in our classrooms and around our schools. But the last thing we really want to do is to have to deal with antisocial and aggressive behavior. Even when the behaviors are subtle and not outwardly physical, but instead verbally abusive or, even more incipient, teasing and bullying through social media, we may become sensitized to our students' unease and discomfort.

Many schools have anti-bullying programs or special events, but there is a need for sustained and sustainable integration of compassionate conflict resolution on a daily basis in the classroom. As teachers, we can engage in the intentional teaching and modeling of compassionate communications skills, regularly, at the classroom level. These communication and conflict resolution skills and practices must be integrated into experiential instruction and our content delivery.

> **Compassionate and respectful interpersonal communication is the backbone of a compassionate classroom and a safe school culture.**

It begins with us—children watch how we handle disruptive or even disrespectful behavior. We believe that it is up to us as educators to ask ourselves these questions when facilitating the resolution of conflicts and dealing with disruptive or aggressive behavior:

- What can be gained from not taking things personally and instead leaning toward kids who are disruptive to assess what is really going on, rather than assuming what is going on?

- How does practicing empathy enable us to assess motive, purpose and reasons for troubling behavior?

- This is about leaning in and learning more before assuming that every difficult encounter is bullying. And it is about teaching our students how to resolve— and prevent—conflicts using compassionate communication.

○ THE HACK: TEACH COMPASSIONATE COMMUNICATION SKILLS ○

What causes conflicts in schools? Conflicts generally arise when one person perceives that there is only one way to meet their need. For example, one student wants what another student has—a toy, a book, a grade, attention, acceptance, being right, feeling better than, and so on. So the student feels frustrated, angry, jealous, sad, annoyed, and tries to meet their needs by acting inappropriately in some way toward the other student—arguing, stealing, becoming verbally or physically abusive, becoming disruptive. Conflicts can occur between students, between students and teachers, between staff members, students and teachers.

The best way to resolve conflicts is to start with self-empathy and empathy. By understanding your own needs and feelings, and what someone's needs are and why they are feeling and behaving the way they are, you can begin to resolve the conflict through compassionate communication. Using design thinking, finding solutions to a problem is founded on empathy, and creating, trying out, and iterating on solutions. Communicating with compassion is also built upon empathy and the ability to take the perspective of the other person with whom you have a conflict.

Compassionate communication involves mindful communication: careful listening to one another, eye contact, reflecting back what each person heard from one another, and practicing empathy. Compassionate and respectful interpersonal communication is the backbone of a compassionate classroom and a safe school culture. These skills can be taught at home and at school, starting at an early age.

In a 19-year longitudinal study that followed the same children from kindergarten through adulthood, researchers from Penn State and Duke University have confirmed what we long suspected and what author Robert Fulghum argued in his book, *All I Need to Know*

I Learned in Kindergarten: The most successful adults are the ones who learned to get along best with their peers in early childhood. Kindergarteners who were helpful and recognized by their teachers for how well they shared, listened to others, and resolved problems with their peers grew up to be well-functioning adults. They were more likely to finish high school, go to college, get and hold jobs, and were less likely to commit crimes and have substance abuse problems or mental health issues. In short, when children learn early in life how to cooperate with others, listen, and resolve conflict, they carry these critical interpersonal communication skills into their adult life.

Strategies for teaching compassionate communication are largely founded on empathy, or recognizing our needs and feelings and those of others. For example, psychologist and peacemaker Marshall Rosenberg developed Nonviolent Communication, which teaches that we can resolve conflicts when we practice self-empathy, empathy for others, and honest self-expression. The premise is that conflicts arise when we don't understand each other's needs, which causes painful or negative feelings such as anger, frustration, annoyance, or fear to arise.

Other compassionate communication approaches emphasize vulnerability and self-compassion, or being willing to risk opening up emotionally to another person. Some methods focus on teaching mindful communication, or the ability to mindfully bring the conversation back to the present moment and to tune into what we need and how we are feeling.

No matter what approach or technique we model or teach proactively, or use in reaction to conflict, we must communicate through our actions and words that what we most value are positive, prosocial relationships with one another in our classrooms and in our schools. That way, we can establish an atmosphere where building relationships, respectful interpersonal communication, and cooperation can not only help to resolve conflicts, but can even work to preempt them.

There are various ways you can teach and model compassionate communication and build your students' conflict resolution skills. Some are proactive activities, and others are strategies to follow in response to conflict or aggressive behavior. Based on our interviews with teachers, and our reading of the research, here are some suggested practices and protocols:

- **HOLD A MORNING MEETING.** One way to establish a peaceful community of respectful learners is to hold a morning meeting. Analogous to what many businesses and organizations do habitually, morning meetings not only set the agenda for the day's work ahead, but also set the tone for communication with one another. This is where students can observe and participate in compassionate communication and learn to build cooperative relationships and listening skills. In schools, morning meetings are most often held at the elementary-school level because their classrooms are generally self-contained. However, the morning meeting format can be incorporated at any grade level. You will find protocols for morning meetings in the supplemental resources section for Hack 10.

- **HAVE ONGOING CONVERSATIONS WITH INDIVIDUAL STUDENTS.** Sometimes called the "Two-by-Ten Strategy," this involves speaking with an individual student for two minutes for 10 consecutive days. In these conversations, the student can talk about anything they want, and the teacher listens mindfully and compassionately. Teachers who have these conversations with at-risk or disruptive students often report that because of this daily compassionate connection with them, their behavior improves dramatically. These regular interpersonal interchanges provide ideal opportunities to model respectful communication using eye contact, reflective listening, and empathy.

- **USE TIME-INS, NOT TIME-OUTS.** Instead of punishing misbehaving students with time-outs by removing them from the classroom, or separating them from the group so they can "think about what they did," consider using a "Time-In." Time-Ins are intended to help students calm down and regain control of themselves, without the shame of punishment and isolation. As opposed to leaving the student to their own devices, in a Time-In the adult may engage calmly with the student by leaning in to find out what is going on. By practicing empathy, the teacher facilitates the student's skill building in communicating compassionately by helping the student identify feelings and distinguish emotions from facts, and investigating the root cause of the trouble. It is important that the teacher chooses their body language carefully—that is, maintains eye contact, modulates the volume and tone of their voice, smiles, and lowers themselves to the student's level—so that they are modeling a respectful conflict resolution stance. They may even choose to tell a story, or use humor, or "I" statements to show the student they empathize with them.

  Often times when there is disruption in the classroom due to conflict between students, or students acting out, these students welcome having a place to go to calm down and cool off. We can offer them a pre-designated "cool off" corner or zone of the room, specifically for Time-Ins or for when students just need a space to process their feelings and disengage from the group but still feel part of the community. These cooling-off corners are also perfect places for us to model ways to collect ourselves by practicing self-compassion through mindful breathing, naming our emotions, giving ourselves permission to be human, and pausing before taking action or attempting to resolve conflicts. Teachers can discuss with their students the purpose of these zones and demonstrate ways to calm down and regain control of ourselves. Pausing has more power than we think.

- **REHEARSE PEACEFUL SOLUTIONS TO CONFLICTS.** Role playing is a good way of teaching students about how to confront one another to resolve conflicts peacefully. It is also a great exercise in empathy. By placing students in a situation where they have to take the opposite side of the conflict, they have to appreciate the other person's point of view and experience what they may be feeling. Teachers can serve as neutral mediators, helping the students choose their words carefully in order to maintain a respectful and compassionate exchange. Role playing facilitates building such conflict resolution skills as: reflective listening, developing creative solutions to disputes, interpersonal communication, self-awareness and self-expression.

- **JOURNAL ABOUT CONFLICTS AND RESOLUTIONS.**
  Journaling about conflicts that our students are
  involved in or have witnessed or read about in
  literature or history books can be a powerful learning
  tool for them. By asking them to reflect and write
  about how they and others felt when the conflict
  occurred, and to track those feelings as the conflict
  was in the resolution phase, they will build empathy.
  They also have the opportunity to try out different
  conflict resolution strategies and process the results.
  When they write about conflicts they may be reading
  about, such as those that actually happened in history
  or fictional conflicts, students can vicariously rehearse
  ways that others have successfully dealt with difficult
  disagreements, differences or feuds. You can ask
  students to write in their journals on a regular or
  periodic basis, or when they are involved in a conflict
  to help with cooling off and finding peaceful solutions.

○ **A BLUEPRINT FOR FULL IMPLEMENTATION** ○

Step 1: Assess your school policies for resolving conflicts.
As you help your students build their conflict resolution skills
through proactive activities and modeling compassionate
communication, it is important for you to familiarize yourself with
your school and your district's policies and practices for resolving
conflicts. These should be clearly stated and available to everyone in
the school community upon request. Ideally, school policies should
be transparent, posted in your classroom, and explained to your
students so that they understand the consequences of their behavior.
The more specific the school policies, the more likely they are to
be followed and reinforced. For example, your school may have a

rubric for aggressive behavior, defining severity levels of physical or verbally abusive behaviors (horseplay, teasing, name-calling, kicking, harassment, and so on) and consequences for first, second, third, and even fourth offenses (apology, call or letter home, silent recess, restitution).

Find out whether your school has any peer mediation training programs or mediation systems in place. In some cases, school counselors are available to provide conflict resolution coaching on a responsive or proactive basis.

Remember that as long as your classroom practices and policies are not in conflict with those of the school where you work, creating an atmosphere of empathy and compassionate communication is in your control. How you teach and model peaceful conflict resolution skills also is under your purview.

Step 2: Determine your school climate type.

Educational institutions vary widely in their school climate types. Some can be characterized by an atmosphere of power and authority, others by a caring and respectful tenor. Organizations such as the National School Climate Center have developed ways to assess school climate as well as provide resources to help school leaders build and sustain healthy and safe schools.

School climate is something students, parents, and visitors can feel when they walk into their school building, or in how they are greeted in the main office—a positive school climate feels inviting and accepting. It is also something you as a teacher or school leader are tuned into when you come to work. How safe or comfortable is the building? How do people get along? What resources are available for instruction?

School culture is more about how teachers and staff work together and their shared values and assumptions. Both school climate and school culture affect student learning, as they have a direct relationship to how safe students feel, emotionally and physically.

The culture you create in your classroom may or may not be in alignment with the climate of your school. As you create and maintain your compassionate classroom, your school will either support your efforts, follow your lead, or push back against you.

As we state throughout this book, we believe that systemic positive transformation starts with you, and in time will permeate your school, and your system, from the ground up.

Step 3: Work with school leaders and school counselors to agree on creating a safe school climate where compassionate communication and nonviolent conflict resolution is the norm.

Start an ongoing discussion about the type of school you all want to work in. How do you want students to feel when they walk in the front door every morning? How do you want parents to feel when they come to volunteer, hold PTA meetings, meet with teachers, administrators, visit the school office or pick up their children? How might you establish a cooperative, collaborative, respectful work environment built on compassionate communication? Empathize, prototype, test, iterate.

Step 4: Establish a school culture where random acts of kindness are the norm.

You might want to consider a 30-day Random Acts of Kindness school-wide challenge. Then extend it to 60 days, and beyond, until kindness becomes the norm of your school community. If every classroom is participating, along with the administrators and staff, you will be setting the stage for transforming your school culture and your school climate. There are lots of great ideas for random acts of kindness online, and even an organization devoted to celebrating a Random Acts of Kindness day. Get creative and inspire your own school community!

◦ OVERCOMING PUSHBACK ◦

We anticipate that you will encounter pushback from those who don't believe that teachers should be addressing conflicts in the classroom but instead should be letting others such as administrative staff charged with dealing with discipline issues take care of these problems. Here are some ways you can respond to them.

We can't afford to lose valuable instructional time to teach conflict resolution skills. We can't afford not to take the time to teach compassionate communication skills. When conflicts arise in the classroom, whether minor or major, between students or between students and faculty, we all must be equipped with conflict resolution skills that are respectful and compassionate. Learning and practicing these skills also preempt escalation of conflicts that are distracting and disruptive to learning and classroom flow.

My school already has conflict resolution and anti-bullying programs. We applaud the school for making strides in addressing the issue of bullying and teasing by holding special events and incorporating various programs and efforts to prevent and resolve conflicts. Many of these programs are effective in raising awareness and teaching skills. However, they rarely are the forces that transform or sustain a positive school culture. Compassionate communication and conflict resolution skills need to be taught and reinforced by teachers' behavior at the classroom level for real positive change to occur and for schools to be healthy and safe.

It's not my job to teach students interpersonal skills. It's outside my scope as a teacher. Whether you know it or not, you are teaching interpersonal skills by setting examples for your students about how to handle conflict. Your behavior and the language you use is a powerful lesson even if you do nothing to proactively teach conflict resolution or actively help your students build their social and emotional skills.

Meg Garofola is an elementary school teacher, currently teaching fourth grade in a highly diverse district in Richmond, Virginia. In her four years of teaching, often in second and third-grade classrooms in neighborhoods characterized by low achievement and extreme poverty, she has been dedicated to teaching her students to be kind and patient. "Compassion has to do with being sensitive to others, so we must practice kindness toward one another. I try to model to students being kind and teaching them to be kind in speech and in their actions," Meg says.

One of the ways she teaches her students to be kind to one another is through the morning meeting she holds with all of her students at the start of each school day. "My morning meeting is centered on creating this community. As we sit in our circle, it gives children an opportunity to express themselves in a social setting, with children their age. It is a safe space . . . where . . . children are asked to listen to others' feelings and experiences." Meg believes that sharing ideas and experiences, along with practicing yoga postures, breath work, and "playing games [focused] on building a family or team" in their daily morning meeting, "cultivates compassion in not only me but my students as well."

What does Meg do if she sees students not practicing kindness? "When students are teasing others or being insensitive, I gently show them another way to interact with their peers." This may even be part of the conversation she has with a difficult student when she practices the "Two-by-Ten" Strategy" of committing to sit down with each student for two minutes for 10 consecutive days. Although the student gets to set the agenda for what they talk about in those two minutes, often they share what's on their mind about conflicts and stressful situations in their lives, and she has the opportunity to address appropriate ways to interact and build peaceful and positive relationships with others.

Meg creates homemade kindness pins with her students and they have the opportunity to recognize each other and wear these pins when they show kindness to one another. She finds this to be a wonderful visible reminder of the values she is trying to teach. At holiday time, Meg turns the idea of gift-giving into a "sharing of self" practice. She asks her students to write down, on a piece of paper that looks like a wrapped present, a gift that each of them has and wants to share with the class. She hangs these presents on a paper tree that is placed on her classroom door for all to see. This year her students gifted each other with such things as "humbleness," "kindness," "tender," "soft spoken," "genuine," "good heart," and "fired up."

Image 10.1: Meg Garofola's students make and wear their heart pins as visible reminders to show one another kindness.

Through her intentional efforts to model and reinforce kindness, cooperation and mindfulness, Meg says that she is creating an atmosphere of compassion and respect where each student comes to believe that they are "valued" and that they "matter." While giving herself permission to be human and practicing self-compassion, Meg's priorities in the classroom are "presence and patience, listening carefully and sensitively, sharing and practicing a growth mindset, practicing kindness, practicing resilience/grit, sharing stories, being flexible and empathetic." She firmly holds onto to the principle that "building compassion starts with compassion for the self."

Reyna Texler teaches a diverse group of first graders at West Haverstraw Elementary School in North Rockland, New York. On many days the children in her class, like too many students in the United States today, come to school hungry, in need of a nap, and a hug, due to disruptive conditions and even traumatic circumstances in their homes. Reyna believes that a significant aspect of her job is to help her students build resilience in order to navigate through challenging times with daily mindfulness practices. Students learn how to self-regulate their emotions by learning the vocabulary to identify sensations, for labeling emotions, and how their feelings connect with their bodies and behaviors. Her school started a school-wide kindness initiative for the month of December. In her classroom, she set her students up to practice kindness by helping them connect what it feels like when they experience the gift of friendship.

Using loving-kindness meditation, a practice Reyna learned while becoming certified as a children's yoga and mindfulness coach, she asked her students to sit comfortably and close their eyes (or lower them if closing their eyes was uncomfortable for them), and to imagine one of their friends walking into the room and sitting nearby. Then she asked them to, quietly and to themselves, offer their friend kind wishes: "May you be happy, may you be healthy, may you be safe, may your life be filled with joy." After they offered these wishes Reyna guided the children to notice what they felt in their bodies when they sent kindness to their friends. One girl said it felt "like a fire burning in her heart." Another said it felt "fuzzy." Then, she asked students to put their thumbs up if they had never experienced this feeling of kindness from a friend. More than half the class put their thumbs up, and those children took a moment to look around, and realized they were not alone. "Thank you for being my friend," a few brave students said to other children with their thumbs up. She invited her class to offer kindness to others that day, and throughout the month—during snack time, when someone needed help, or before or after school. "It's our job now to bring kind words to those children." Reyna noticed frequent spontaneous expressions of kindness all around, and heard students say to one another, "You're a good friend. I want you to know that."

Reyna considers school climate to be "the hidden curriculum." She notes that "it isn't on paper listed under any learning standard yet, but Emotional Intelligence needs to be taught . . . to teach children how to be kind, how to be empathetic . . . how to raise morale . . . and not only how to do it for your kids but also how kids do it for other kids in the classroom."

Image 10.2: Reyna Texler's students practicing loving-kindness meditation as part of a school-wide kindness challenge.

Megan and Reyna are just two examples of teachers who are hacking school culture, one learner and one classroom at a time. Inspired by their own practices of self-compassion and kindness, and committed to creating an atmosphere of positivity resonance, they are teaching their children to tune into their positive emotions, share them with others, and to build a community of sensitivity and cooperation. And these children are taking those skills with them to the larger community, and into their future relationships.

Are you ready to begin explicitly teaching nonviolent communication and compassionate conflict resolution? You will find an array of articles and protocols in the supplemental resources folder for Hack 10:

- Protocols for conflict resolution, including nonviolent communication
- Reference for study that followed kids from kindergarten through adulthood
- Links to ways to assess school climate
- Links to organizations to connect with around kindness challenges
- More from Meg Garofola and Reyna Texler

Supplemental resources for Hack 10

CONCLUSION

You must be the change you wish to see in the world.
—MAHATMA GANDHI

Bullying, teasing, social media shaming and harassment, violence, aggression, and disrespectful acts and language are real phenomena in schools today. These are real behavior problems that require real behavior solutions—as are anxiety and depression and other mental health ills.

We're all looking for solutions. The faster, the better.

So, what about bullying prevention programs, character-building programs, and incentive-based initiatives intended to curb anti-social behavior and bring people together? These seem like efficient ways to get traction. Isn't that what hacking school culture is all about? Doing what's fast and easy?

Not at all.

Don't get us wrong; we have no problem with those approaches, but the teachers and administrators that we support often tell us they just aren't enough. And of course they aren't. Theoretical models of behavioral change validate our own observations and experiences; human beings evolve slowly, over time. Change requires quite a bit of pre-contemplation, preparation, supported action, and dedicated maintenance.

Assemblies, posters, morning announcements, contests, mnemonics, awards, and quick readings about character development might support the work of cultural shift, but they're no replacement for it. They simply aren't enough.

We believe that compassionate schools are built one learner and teacher and classroom at a time. Shift begins to happen the moment we start treating ourselves with kindness. This makes us more empathetic toward our students. It continues as we assess their interests and needs and offer them more space at our curriculum-planning tables. When we help young people see themselves and others in all of their beautiful complexities, we inspire them to value diversity and seek it out with intention. When we teach them how to extinguish shame and blame, we empower them to manage their own baggage in ways that make them trigger-proof.

This isn't the work of a single event or even of string of them. It's about becoming more human with our students, and then deciding who we will stand beside and what we will stand for.

It's one thing to invite a powerful speaker with a riveting story to inspire students and staff. Once that speaker leaves, the real work begins, though. How might we give people the tools they need to follow in that speaker's footsteps? What are the protocols? Which practices work best? How do we bridge the distance between inspiring our students and empowering them to practice compassion—explicitly? Any compelling speaker can hand any member of an audience a pair of rose-colored glasses. How do we ensure that they aren't discarded on the way out the door? More importantly, when will everyone have the opportunity to put those lenses on again and again and again, in order to continue seeing the world we hope to create? And who is going to help kids get there? How?

The classroom is the perfect arena for this kind of learning and growth. It's here that we come to learn and work together, peering into history and literature and current events. In the classroom, students can wrestle with ambivalence and discomfort. They can role-play and engage in simulations that challenge their assumptions. They can plan to change, test new ideas, and give themselves permission to be human. They can pull those glasses on and off, push against both views, and name what they see in their current realities.

The classroom is the place where our learning about compassion is sustained over time.

Do we believe that assemblies and contests and celebrations of growth are important? They can be, certainly. What matters most is the real work, though.

And that happens one learner, one teacher, and one classroom at a time.

If these ideas compel or challenge you, you know that you aren't alone. We'd love to hear from you. Reach out to @AngelaStockman or @EllenFeigGray on Twitter. Let's talk more about what it means to hack school culture and create compassionate classrooms.

OTHER BOOKS IN THE HACK LEARNING SERIES

HACKING EDUCATION
10 Quick Fixes for Every School
By Mark Barnes (@markbarnes19) and
Jennifer Gonzalez (@cultofpedagogy)

In the bestselling *Hacking Education*, Mark Barnes and Jennifer Gonzalez employ decades of teaching experience and hundreds of discussions with education thought leaders to show you how to find and hone the quick fixes that every school and classroom need. Using a Hacker's mentality, they provide **one Aha moment after another** with 10 Quick Fixes For Every School—a solutions to everyday problems and teaching methods that any teacher or administrator can implement immediately.

"Barnes and Gonzalez don't just solve problems; they turn teachers into hackers—a transformation that is right on time."
—**DON WETTRICK**, AUTHOR OF *PURE GENIUS*

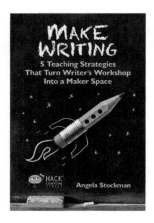

MAKE WRITING
5 Teaching Strategies That Turn Writer's Workshop Into a Maker Space
By Angela Stockman (@angelastockman)

Everyone's favorite education blogger and writing coach, Angela Stockman, turns teaching strategies and practices upside down in the bestselling, *Make Writing*. She spills you out of your chair, shreds your lined paper, and launches you and your writer's workshop into the maker space! Stockman provides five right-now writing strategies that reinvent instruction and **inspire both young and adult writers** to express ideas with tools that have rarely, if ever, been considered. *Make Writing* is a fast-paced journey inside Stockman's Western New York Young Writer's Studio, alongside the students there who learn how to write and how to make, employing Stockman's unique teaching methods.

"Offering suggestions for using new materials in old ways, thoughtful questions, and specific tips for tinkering and finding new audiences, this refreshing book is inspiring and practical in equal measure."

—AMY LUDWIG VANDERWATER, AUTHOR AND TEACHER

HACKING ASSESSMENT
10 Ways to Go Gradeless in a Traditional Grades School
By Starr Sackstein (@mssackstein)

In the bestselling *Hacking Assessment,* award-winning teacher and world-renowned formative assessment expert Starr Sackstein unravels one of education's oldest mysteries: How to assess learning without grades—even in a school that uses numbers, letters, GPAs, and report cards. While many educators can only muse about the possibility of a world without grades, teachers like Sackstein are **reimagining education**. In this unique, eagerly-anticipated book, Sackstein shows you exactly how to create a remarkable no-grades classroom like hers, a vibrant place where students grow, share, thrive, and become independent learners who never ask, "What's this worth?"

"The beauty of the book is that it is not an empty argument against grades—but rather filled with valuable alternatives that are practical and will help to refocus the classroom on what matters most."

—**Adam Bellow**, White House Presidential Innovation Fellow

HACKING THE COMMON CORE
10 Strategies for Amazing Learning in a Standardized World
By Michael Fisher (@fisher1000)

In *Hacking the Common Core,* longtime teacher and CCSS specialist Mike Fisher shows you how to bring fun back to learning, with 10 amazing hacks for teaching all Core subjects, while engaging students and making learning fun. Fisher's experience and insights help teachers and parents better understand close reading, balancing fiction and nonfiction, using projects with the Core, and much more. *Hacking the Common Core* provides **read-tonight-implement-tomorrow strategies** for teaching the standards in fun and engaging ways, improving teaching and learning for students, parents, and educators.

HACKING LEADERSHIP

10 Ways Great Leaders Inspire Learning That Teachers, Students, and Parents Love

By Joe Sanfelippo (@joesanfelippoFC) and Tony Sinanis (@tonysinanis)

In the runaway bestseller *Hacking Leadership*, renowned school leaders Joe Sanfelippo and Tony Sinanis bring readers inside schools that few stakeholders have ever seen—places where students not only come first but have a unique voice in teaching and learning. Sanfelippo and Sinanis ignore the bureaucracy that stifles many leaders, focusing instead on building a culture of **engagement, transparency, and most important, fun.** *Hacking Leadership* has superintendents, principals, and teacher leaders around the world employing strategies they never before believed possible.

"The authors do a beautiful job of helping leaders focus inward, instead of outward. This is an essential read for leaders who are, or want to lead, learner-centered schools."

—GEORGE COUROS, AUTHOR OF THE INNOVATOR'S MINDSET

HACKING LITERACY
5 Ways To Turn Any Classroom Into a Culture Of Readers
By Gerard Dawson (@gerarddawson3)

In *Hacking Literacy*, classroom teacher, author, and reading consultant Gerard Dawson reveals 5 simple ways any educator or parent can turn even the most reluctant reader into a thriving, enthusiastic lover of books. Dawson cuts through outdated pedagogy and standardization, turning reading theory into practice, sharing **valuable reading strategies**, and providing what *Hack Learning Series* readers have come to expect—actionable, do-it-tomorrow strategies that can be built into long-term solutions.

HACKING ENGAGEMENT
50 Tips & Tools to Engage Teachers and Learners Daily
By James Alan Sturtevant (@jamessturtevant)

Some students hate your class. Others are just bored. Many are too nice, or too afraid, to say anything about it. Don't let it bother you; it happens to the best of us. But now, it's **time to engage!** In *Hacking Engagement*, the seventh book in the *Hack Learning Series*, veteran high school teacher, author, and popular podcaster James Sturtevant provides 50—that's right, five-oh—tips and tools that will engage even the most reluctant learners daily.

HACKING HOMEWORK
10 Strategies That Inspire Learning Outside the Classroom
By Starr Sackstein (@mssackstein) and
Connie Hamilton (@conniehamilton)

Learning outside the classroom is being reimagined, and student engagement is better than ever. World-renowned author/educator Starr Sackstein has changed how teachers around the world look at traditional grades. Now she's teaming with veteran educator, curriculum director, and national presenter Connie Hamilton to bring you **10 powerful strategies** for teachers and parents that promise to inspire independent learning at home, without punishments or low grades.

"Starr Sackstein and Connie Hamilton have assembled a book full of great answers to the question, 'How can we make homework engaging and meaningful?'"

        —**DOUG FISHER AND NANCY FREY**, AUTHORS AND PRESENTERS

HACKING PROJECT BASED LEARNING

10 Easy Steps to PBL and Inquiry in the Classroom

By Ross Cooper (@rosscoops31) and Erin Murphy (@murphysmusings5)

As questions and mysteries around PBL and inquiry continue to swirl, experienced classroom teachers and school administrators Ross Cooper and Erin Murphy have written a book that will empower those intimidated by PBL to cry, "I can do this!" while at the same time providing added value for those who are already familiar with the process. *Hacking Project Based Learning* demystifies what PBL is all about with **10 hacks that construct a simple path** that educators and students can easily follow to achieve success.

"*Hacking Project Based Learning* is a classroom essential. Its ten simple 'hacks' will guide you through the process of setting up a learning environment in which students will thrive from start to finish."

—**Daniel H. Pink**, *New York Times* Bestselling Author of *DRIVE*

HACK LEARNING ANTHOLOGY
Innovative Solutions for Teachers and Leaders
Edited by Mark Barnes (@markbarnes19)

Anthology brings you the most innovative education Hacks from the first nine books in the *Hack Learning Series*. Written by twelve award-winning classroom teachers, principals, superintendents, college instructors, and international presenters, *Anthology* is every educator's new problem-solving handbook. It is both a preview of nine other books and a **full-fledged, feature-length blueprint** for solving your biggest school and classroom problems.

HACKING GOOGLE FOR EDUCATION
99 Ways to Leverage Google Tools in Classrooms, Schools, and Districts

By Brad Currie (@bradmcurrie), Billy Krakower (@wkrakower), and Scott Rocco (@ScottRRocco)

If you could do more with Google than search, what would it be? Would you use Google Hangouts to connect students to cultures around the world? Would you finally achieve a paperless workflow with Classroom? Would you inform and engage stakeholders district-wide through Blogger? Now, you can say Yes to all of these, because Currie, Krakower, and Rocco remove the limits in Hacking Google for Education, giving you **99 Hacks in 33 chapters**, covering Google in a unique way that benefits all stakeholders.

"Connected educators have long sought a comprehensive resource for implementing blended learning with G Suite. *Hacking Google for Education* superbly delivers with a plethora of classroom-ready solutions and linked exemplars."

—DR. ROBERT R. ZYWICKI, SUPERINTENDENT OF WEEHAWKEN TOWNSHIP SCHOOL DISTRICT

HACKING ENGAGEMENT AGAIN
50 Teacher Tools That Will Make Students Love Your Class
By James Alan Sturtevant (@jamessturtevant)

50 Student Engagement Hacks just weren't enough. Thirty-three-year veteran classroom teacher, James Alan Sturtevant, wowed teachers with the original Hacking Engagement, which contained 50 Tips and Tools to Engage Teachers and Learners Daily. Those educators and students got better, but they craved more. So, longtime educator and wildly popular student engager Sturtevant is *Hacking Engagement Again*!

This book is packed with ideas that can be implemented right away: Some creatively weave technology into instruction, others are just plain creative, and all of them are smart. Plus, the QR codes take the reader to so many more fantastic resources. With this book in hand, every teacher will find ways to freshen up their teaching and make it fun again!"

—JENNIFER GONZALEZ, BESTSELLING AUTHOR, SPEAKER,
AND CEO AT CULTOFPEDAGOGY.COM

HACKING DIGITAL LEARNING STRATEGIES
10 Ways to Launch EdTech Missions in Your Classroom
By Shelly Sanchez Terrell (@ShellTerrell)

In *Hacking Digital Learning Strategies*, international EdTech presenter and NAPW Woman of the Year Shelly Sanchez Terrell demonstrates the power of EdTech Missions--lessons and projects that inspire learners to use web tools and social media to innovate, research, collaborate, problem-solve, campaign, crowd fund, crowdsource, and publish. The 10 Missions in *Hacking DLS* are more than enough to transform how teachers integrate technology, but there's also much more here. Included in the book is a **38-page Mission Toolkit**, complete with reproducible mission cards, badges, polls, and other handouts that you can copy and distribute to students immediately.

"The secret to Shelly's success as an education collaborator on a global scale is that she shares information most revered by all educators, information that is original, relevant, vetted, and proven, combining technology with proven education methodology in the classroom. This book provides relevance to a 21st century educator."

—THOMAS WHITBY, AUTHOR, PODCASTER, BLOGGER, CONSULTANT, CO-FOUNDER OF #EDCHAT

HACKING PARENTHOOD
10 Mantras You Can Use Daily to Reduce the
Stress of Parenting
By Kimberley Moran (@kimberleygmoran)

You throw out consequences willy-nilly. You're tired of solutions that are all or nothing. You're frustrated with the daily chaos. Enter mantras, invaluable parenting anchors wrapped in tidy packages. These will become your go-to tools to calm your mind, focus your parenting, and concentrate on what you want for your kids. Kimberley Moran is a parent and a teacher who works tirelessly to find best practices for simplifying parenting and maximizing parent-child communication. Using **10 Parent Mantras as cues to stop time and reset**, Moran shares concrete ways to parent with intention and purpose, without losing your cool.

HACKING CLASSROOM MANAGEMENT
10 Ideas To Help You Become the Type
of Teacher They Make Movies About
By Mike Roberts (@baldroberts)

Utah English Teacher of the Year and sought-after speaker Mike Roberts brings you 10 quick and easy classroom management hacks that will make your classroom the place to be for all your students. He shows you how to create an amazing learning environment that actually makes discipline, rules and consequences obsolete, no matter if you're a new teacher or a thirty-year veteran teacher.

"Mike writes from experience; he's learned, sometimes the hard way, what works and what doesn't, and he shares those lessons in this fine little book. The book is loaded with specific, easy-to-apply suggestions that will help any teacher create and maintain a classroom where students treat one another with respect, and where they learn."

—CHRIS CROWE, ENGLISH PROFESSOR AT BYU,
PAST PRESIDENT OF ALAN, AUTHOR OF *DEATH COMING UP THE HILL*,
*GETTING AWAY WITH MURDER: THE TRUE STORY OF THE EMMETT TILL
CASE; MISSISSIPPI TRIAL, 1955*; AND MANY OTHER YA BOOKS

Hack Learning Resources

All Things Hack Learning:

hacklearning.org

The Entire Hack Learning Series on Amazon:

hacklearningbooks.com

The Hack Learning Podcast, hosted by Mark Barnes:

hacklearningpodcast.com

Hack Learning on Twitter

@HackMyLearning

#HackLearning

#HackingLeadership

#HackingLiteracy

#HackingEngagement

#HackingHomework

#HackingPBL

#MakeWriting

#HackGoogleEdu

#EdTechMissions

#ParentMantras

#MovieTeacher

#CompassionateClassrooms

Hack Learning on Facebook:

facebook.com/hacklearningseries

Hack Learning on Instagram:

hackmylearning

The Hack Learning Academy:

hacklearningacademy.com

About the Authors

Angela Stockman is a writer, teacher, and professional learning service provider. Over the last decade, she's supported teachers of writing in over seventy different school districts throughout the United States and Canada. Angela's areas of expertise include curriculum design, instructional coaching, formative assessment design, standards-based grading, and pedagogical documentation. The author of *Make Writing: 5 Strategies That Turn Writer's Workshop into a Maker Space*, Angela founded The WNY Young Writers' Studio, a community of writers and teachers of writing in western New York State.

She enjoys helping other school and community leaders design, launch, and sustain similar spaces within and beyond the four walls of their schools. Angela has taught at the graduate level, she has supervised student teachers, and she has lea curriculum and assessment design initiatives inside of multiple university departments. She also works with business and nonprofit leaders to craft and share meaningful narratives about the organizations they serve. You may find Angela on Twitter, Facebook, LinkedIn, and Google+. She also blogs in her own space: www.angelastockman.com.

Ellen Feig Gray began her career forty years ago as a developmental psychology researcher, and since then has been applying relevant findings from positive psychology, communications, and the science of happiness and well-being, to support parents and others who raise and educate children and teens. She has used her expertise to advocate for young people in various ways, including developing policies and practices for television broadcasts, advertising guidelines, marketing communications campaigns, as well as working with nonprofit organizations. As founder of Parent with Perspective she provides practical wisdom and expert advice, through coaching, workshops, talks, blog posts and articles. Connect with Ellen at www.parentwithperspective.com and on Twitter @EllenFeigGray.

PUBLICATIONS

Times 10 is a helping all education stakeholders improve every aspect of teaching and learning. We are committed to solving big problems with simple ideas. We bring you content from experts, shared through multiple channels, including books, podcasts, and an array of social networks. Our mantra is simple: Read it today; fix it tomorrow. Stay in touch with us at HackLearning.org, at #HackLearning on Twitter, and on the Hack Learning Facebook group.